S. H. E.

S. H. E.

Share · Heal · Empower.™

Collected Journeys

Paired with Artwork

VOLUME ONE

Compiled and Composed

by

SHANNON HOGAN COHEN

DECKLE WAY PRESS

DECKLE WAY PRESS

Deckle Way Press

1155 Camino Del Mar, Suite 116

Del Mar, California, USA 92014

"Sharing stories — one uneven page at a time."

www.DeckleWayPress.com

Ordering Information: Special discounts are available on quantity purchases by corporations, associations, and others. For details, contact the publisher. Orders by U.S. trade bookstores and wholesalers.

Please visit www.ShareHealEmpower.com

Library of Congress Cataloging in Publication Data:

ISBN (paperback): 978-1-7320335-1-1

ISBN (ebook): 978-1-7320335-2-8

Library of Congress Control Number: 2018902026

1. Women's Non-Fiction 2.Inspiration & Motivation 3. Personal Growth

First edition, Volume One 2018

Printed in the United States of America

10 9 8 7 6 5 4 3 2 1

Cover and Interior Design Production: Sharon Belknap Design

S.H.E. Logo: Shelby Hogan Kovac

To

all women worldwide

who embody perseverance, unimaginable human spirit

and rock solid resilience,

especially my mother,

Joni

CONTENTS

FOREWORD

We all need candles to light our path in life. Let this book be your guide and your inspiration. *Share Heal Empower* is a gem filled with the stories of "SHEROS," twenty-four extraordinary women who can teach us how to shine, laugh, accept and endure through life's great losses and challenges. Their courage and spirit will lift you and connect you to one fascinating woman after another. The magic, messages and moments in *S.H.E.* will stay in your heart for a very long time.

Shannon Hogan Cohen has brilliantly brought together a unique and diverse group of brave women, linked through their difficulties, personal power and resilience. I applaud every woman who trusted her own inner guidance. Leilah, who suffered physical and emotional abuse tells us, "Be the sunshine when the light cannot be found."

These wise women's stories are more than just important. Storytelling is one of the most ancient soul-retrieving arts. In fact, if you are no longer touched and inspired by stories, it is actually a sign of soul loss; this is true for your own story as well.

Each of us has a story. No woman's story is too small to make a difference in the world. Sharing our stories is *big healing medicine*, leading us to acknowledge who we are truly meant to be. The stories told in this book work on us from the inside out, taking us to places we cannot get to on our own. They help us access a place of deeper compassion and empathy.

Challenges hold gifts. Often the challenge *is* the *gift* as we read and then integrate each woman's powerful, profound and moving story. Despite some having the lack of support from significant others in their lives, the women in this book continued past their obstacles until they arrived at their authentic place in the world. The tales of their insights, triumphs and breakthroughs support us in finding hope for our own dark times. We can then recognize we are never, ever alone. We need inspiration, but most of all we need each other.

Shannon Hogan Cohen offers you the best of stories. Driven by her own deep longing to connect with remarkable women, she took a journey, embarked on a quest for the most meaningful life stories she could find. She now places these wonders at our feet, like a candle offering to illuminate our path and light up our soul.

Terry Laszlo-Gopadze is an award-winning author, storyteller and Licensed Marriage and Family Therapist. She is also the editor of the book, *The Spirit of a Woman: Stories to Empower and Inspire.*

ACKNOWLEDGEMENTS

I could have never completed this book, without the help and support of many people.

Let the crowd-pandering begin...

Cheers to the twenty-four fearless women tucked inside these pages, and the twenty-four altruistic artists who've illustrated their images. Without each one of you and your individual inspiration, this book would not have been possible.

∽

To my Franken-brain, you know who you are. Without you and your invaluable advice and developmental editing abilities, these stories would not be architecturally solid.

∽

Thanks to Rabia Tredeau, aka Saint Rabia—needless to say, this book would never have had the "smoothness" it does as a result of your editing. You came into my life at the most opportune time, reinvigorating me both personally and professionally (thank you, Michelle Marchildon).

∽

A nod to Bobbie & Jed Cohen for your keen grammatical skill set and for always picking up the phone.

To Sharon Belknap, your "tidbits of love" throughout this process kept me well-balanced. As a gifted graphic designer, amazing artist, and expert in your field, I am so grateful you showed up and said, "YES," at Claire's on Cedros. You were vital in the layout and design, not to mention taking extra time to make S.H.E. come to life.

∾

To my sissy, Shelby Anner. I have the utmost respect for you. Aside from the random talk therapy sessions over FaceTime (thanks Binky, Mila & Teo for sharing her), along with winning the title contest, crafting the logo, guidance on artwork, and above all, for being a trusted comrade throughout this entire process. I am sorry for beating you up when we were younger. (Are you happy now? It is officially in print!)

∾

Additional appreciation also goes to my doulas. Each of you have cheered me on throughout the birthing of this book's journey: Brittany Jo - your sister support, Gina - your leading light, Amanda - your ability to connect, Tristen - your intuitive insight, Esmeralda - your translation, Sherrie - your exceptional organization, Linda (Lila) - your playful energy and Paige - our whine time.

∾

To my mother, Joni…for whom the impetus of this book was derived. Your suffering and sacrifice over the years never went unnoticed. It is your time to shine now, Mommy. I love you!

Acknowledgements

To my two teenage sons and extremely influential young men in my life, Cody and Cole; in no specific order, receive a special thank you from me. You are the center of my heart; being your mom has taught me to love deeply. I will continue to keep candy in my babe cave as bait. Let this be the first book you both read in its entirety.

∾

Last, but by no means least: the most influential mature man in my life: TC. You have the ability to edit my existence in a way that softens my verbose nature, all the while mastering the art of "Happy wife; Happy life." Thank you for tolerating my crazy. I am eternally grateful.

∾

As I flailed forward at times with jazz hands, I am thankful to all those who have offered encouragement and support along the way.

INTRODUCTION

I went to sleep a child and woke up someone I was not ready to be.

At age eleven, I never expected to lose my thirty-year-old father. Growing up in a small farming township in Michigan, we were a community of close-knit people who valued their families, hard work and weekends.

I savor my childhood memories. I look back on playing tag with the neighborhood boys until dusk; then hiding in the pussy willow tree behind the garage, hearing my parents hollering for me to come home—and ignoring them, of course!

I remember watching firefly lightshows during summer nights, those tiny luminescent insects bringing on-the-spot magic with their flickering and fading sparks. I would cut the long grass in front of our house on humid summer days, then ride my purple Schwinn bike with its floral banana seat to the local dairy bar for a treat. To this day, the aroma of a freshly cut lawn makes me crave a soft-serve ice cream cone dripping with chocolate coating.

I do not miss those pesky mosquitoes. I loved the smell of autumn leaves burning and delighted in throwing handfuls of chestnuts into the flames, as I listened for the crackle and pop. Sledding down snowy hills and racing snowmobiles was my wintertime fun. All these reminiscences evoke my inner child's recollections and imaginings.

My parents were just kids themselves on that dark June night. An act of exploration and young love—not necessarily romantic, but memorable, a first for both my mother and father who were both seventeen. Yet, neither one had a clear vision for the future. Nevertheless, I arrived nine months later.

My memories of my father and mother being together were limited. What a family should be was never defined out loud. I assumed everything that happened in our house was normal, yet what really is normal? One time, I watched my father throw a pillow at my mother to intentionally collapse the newspaper she was holding while she was reading it—this little episode may offer an insight into his silliness, as well as her seriousness.

Truth be told, when we were together I was certainly influenced by his passion for life and his "no rules" approach. We had fun together, possibly because our relationship was designed that way. My mother always took on the responsible role, which to this day I thank and admire her for doing. She did her best to safeguard me and create a stable environment.

I cherish the memories I accumulated the last few years of my father's life. Allowing me to be his beautician, I would place countless clips on his curly hair and beard while he watched television. My mother's all-time favorite pet peeve was when he would answer the telephone by saying, "Yeah?" instead of the time-honored, "Hello?" Tagging along with him on a spontaneous drive in his Chevy truck, I would sit on the Indian blanket seat cover, filled with anticipation. Mom never approved of his impulsiveness. We wouldn't tell her where we went or what we ate on our adventures.

On Christmas morning in 1984, Mom had bought my father a traditional camouflage-hunting outfit that included pants and jacket. I distinctly remember her taking a picture of him all dressed up. Then he sat back down into his tan lazy boy recliner, looked up at her matter-of-factly, and said, "I will not need this."

We had a short run together, my father and I. Although brief, it was unforgettable.

Until the moment it happened, the idea of losing my father never entered my mind, even though he had been sick for two years. I remember hearing the telephone ring at 6:26 AM. My aunt answered the phone, and only minutes later she grimly told my sister and me, "Your father has died of cancer." It was such a stark change from the predictability of our life up to that point. That unexpected difference in the family dynamic forced me to grow up very quickly. I always knew the life and death cycle occurs around us naturally, but I was awakened to this force when my "adored father" died. Unable to articulate my grief, I suppressed the tears and pain of a confused child for decades.

My father's death, his relationship with my mother, along with my own relationship with her, impacted me in ways that I never thought possible. Growing up, I realized my mother did not have the emotional capacity to nurture herself, let alone me and my younger sister. I learned to silently deal with things on my own, forging ahead, while feeling forsaken and isolated from love.

Throughout my life I've struggled with feelings of abandonment, which caused major collateral damage for my relationships with both women and men. My desire to be independent and self-sufficient, almost to a fault, was deeply rooted in my mother's emotional neglect after my dad died. Of course, I never realized any of this at the time.

It took me years to put the jagged puzzle pieces together. Life offered me clues to help solve my puzzle, but I ignored them. Graduating from college, working and traveling in the corporate world, marrying a true gentleman, and raising two active boys have kept me busy. I liked being in constant motion; it was easier to avoid remembering and then reflecting on my past. From the outside, everything appeared to be perfect. My inside, though, was telling me that something was missing.

I started searching for someone, anyone, who felt the same way. That's when life began to place courageous, open-hearted women in my path. At a time when I was feeling empty and looking for answers, their stories, along with the wisdom that naturally followed, gave me a sense of both courage and camaraderie that I had never known.

I discovered my vulnerability created a safe space where other women felt secure enough to be the same. Our exchanges brought healing to a whole new level as we shared, grieved, learned, and eventually moved forward together.

S.H.E. was born in that spirit of sisterhood.

This is a collection of some—yet certainly not all—of the women who have honored me with their profound stories. Writing this book has been a life-changing adventure, blessing me with countless new friendships along the way. Often after meeting a kindred spirit and hearing her story, she would casually comment, "I have a friend you must meet—you should hear her story, too!"

So through an organic course of introductions and meetings, this compilation of twenty-four narratives came together. I was able to sit down personally with each woman (with the exception of one), and we chatted, laughed, cried—sometimes over the course of several days. For some, the remembrances came easily, their battle scars worn proudly for the world to see. Others took more time to warm up; they kept their secrets closely guarded, the way life often teaches us to do.

I've presented their heartfelt stories, garnered from hours of interviews and many follow-up emails, as if they were speaking directly to you, the reader, thus including you more intimately in the sacred circle of trust that was formed between us.

This circle of friends expanded even further with the addition of a unique, individualized work of art for each woman featured in the book. Twenty-four passionate artists were mindfully paired with their warrior women storytellers based on similar interests or struggles, to graciously create an original art piece inspired by each narrator's journey. In many cases, the artist was able to speak to "her" woman personally, forming a genuine connection of their own.

S.H.E. has now become a community of almost fifty women and continues to grow. These extraordinary connections have created healing and happiness in my heart, and I trust they will do the same for others who read these stories. My hope is that this book will encourage and inspire people of all ages to start sharing and learning from each other.

It's the beginning of a powerful conversation...

Chapter One

Dalia

Both the aqua de limon *(limeade), and a thatched roof were useful today, since the Mexico sun was shining brightly on us during International Women's Day. I was thrilled to be celebrating Dalia, and felt it appropriate to be sharing time with two tenacious females. Anna, a dear friend, had introduced us and helped translate my conversation at her beachfront home in Puerto Escondido. Dalia has known Anna and her family for eight years; both have been influential in each other's lives on countless levels.*

We had just met the day before. My broken Spanish provided a bit of communication between us, besides just smiles and hugs. Today, after a few moments, our awkwardness quickly dissipated with proper interpretation, while Dalia and her mother, Maria, tried to teach me the ways of their culinary brilliance. I can still see Dalia's jet black hair pulled back smoothly in a bun as she giggled under her breath watching my incompetent attempt at making sopes, *a traditional Mexican dish with a thick tortilla made with* masa *(corn).*

Dalia was adorned with an embroidered Puebla peasant blouse in a vibrant floral design that was an unforgettable work of needlepoint. Her timely perseverance in teaching me to cook seemed to be the key to unlocking personal freedom. She came prepared for the interview with a notebook and pen, and after our kitchen experience, she was poised and ready as we sat under a traditional palapa. Dalia never shied away from being both bold and honest, which made our emotional four-hour conversation even more extraordinary. She is a shining example of resilience in the face of tragedy.

We laughed and cried together while she shared many memories of her life, both as a playful young girl and as a mature woman now in her thirties. I noticed her soulful dark brown eyes sparkle as she looked to the heavens seemingly for both strength and calm during our lengthy conversation. Her story reminds me that sometimes we must lose something to gain something.

On my last night with Dalia, pan de elote, a type of sweet cornbread dessert, was the perfect finish and topper to her bittersweet mole sauce surrounding the flavorful chicken. During my time with Dalia, I learned two more family secrets: There is no quick or strict way to make a twenty-eight-ingredient mole rojo sauce, and there is no time limit, nor one right way to grieve.

The idea of committing suicide was in stark, bleak contrast to my brightly colored days as an adolescent girl.

My childhood was simple, full of fun and games. Playing pranks on classmates was a favorite pastime. Peddling my father's fish, typically *ojotones*, a googly-eyed baitfish, gave me money and independence as a child. To tell the truth, I was a little mischievous as well, sometimes "relocating" roses from neighbors' gardens and selling them to other neighbors, when I didn't give a few to my mother as a gift.

I was also bit rebellious and wore short skirts, even when my father forbade me to do so. In fact, this was how I captured the attention of my future husband, Ruben, at a *tortilleria,* a local eatery that made and sold tortillas. At fifteen, wearing a miniskirt made snug from all the cornmeal l had consumed, I married Ruben with his dark, deep eyes and dimples. We had a beautiful daughter together, Jessie.

The blissful life I had imagined changed suddenly when I discovered my husband had been cheating on me with other women here in town. At the time, I was pregnant with our second daughter, Mayra. I told him to leave, so he moved to Kentucky to find work. Although we had never divorced, he married another woman and had a child with her.

I survived those early years without him. It was a tough time having a baby alone, and then raising both girls by myself. Each had her unique personality. Jessie was quiet; Mayra was spirited. It turned out, it was not only me raising them; they became my motivation to grow.

I had to be creative to find ways to make money. I was a waitress, then a gas station attendant. Once the owners at the gas station realized my capabilities, they moved me into an office position. The tips were much better pumping gas, but I needed stability and insurance for me and my daughters.

After four years, Ruben returned from Kentucky, and my parents insisted I work it out with my estranged husband. Divorce was not an option. He had been back almost one year, when Mayra stopped acting like her feisty self. I took her to have a series of tests to see if she was sick.

On May 8, 2008, my spunky six-year-old was diagnosed with lymphatic cancer, Burkitt lymphoma, a very rare form of non-Hodgkin lymphoma. Every day was nerve-racking. In the hospital, I watched the doctors extract spinal fluid, which was very painful and hard on her already distressed body. I felt helpless seeing my child suffer. Still, I was hopeful this deadly disease could be cured with the intensive chemotherapy she endured for a wrenching nine months. We went back and forth to Oaxaca City for her treatments, usually an eight- to ten-hour bus ride, every other week on very winding roads.

Neither Ruben nor I were working, and the medical bills were enormous. We tried as many treatments, cultural cures, and therapeutic interventions as we could find and afford. It was so stressful watching her suffer. I was never mad at God; I prayed daily and even tried making a deal with Him.

Mayra came home from Oaxaca City in December 2008. Tests showed no more cancerous cells. She was feeling better, but her remission was short-lived. My fears and concerns came back with a vengeance when she began to feel sick to her stomach. It had only been three days since we had brought her home. We took her to our local hospital, and the doctor told us we must transfer Mayra immediately to another hospital an hour away, because they did not have the correct medical equipment. This was at 5:30 PM.

I was desperate, and then became hysterical trying to find a way to get Mayra to the hospital when we were told the town's ambulance was not working. I was frantically trying to find transportation for my dying child. I could not even get the firemen to take her. A family member finally came with their car to take us. We arrived in the middle of a shift change. The nurses were rude, telling me to shut up and wait. My baby girl was in extreme pain, and there was nothing I could do except plead for the attention and care she needed.

I felt powerless.

These disrespectful and ignorant people were not the ones I wanted treating my sick child, but I pleaded and begged for them to give my daughter the attention she needed. Finally, fifteen minutes later, the doctor came in and gave her an IV for pain. At that moment as her mother, I knew this was the end.

On December 11, 2008 at 7 PM, my entire life stopped with the death of my baby girl, Mayra Sanchez Lopez. Swaddling my limp child's body close to me, I was numb.

The hospital noise was gone and everything around me became a blur. I only saw my precious Mayra. All I could do was kiss her face, gently stroking her silky black hair. Her skin felt warm, and her eyes were closed as she painlessly lay in my arms wrapped in a hospital blanket. I kept thinking that both of us would wake from this bad dream, that she would open those twinkling brown eyes and come back to me.

Holding your dead child is horrific. I could not let her go. I prayed to God my strong-willed child would begin to stir, and that we would be back together. But she never moved.

It felt as if I had come to the end of myself. I was in shock. There was nothing left for me. When I returned home, unable to be a mother to my older daughter, Jessie, I could barely get through the days. I could not touch any of Mayra's dolls in her room for over a year; everything stayed exactly the way she left it.

I felt lost and had many dark times after her death.

Ladies from church visited me every Friday, even if I was not in the mood to talk. I went to therapy. I worked on re-establishing my relationship with my oldest daughter. I learned she had become envious of the attention Mayra received. Jessie also told me that she had never given Mayra a hug or said goodbye. When her six-year-old little sister died, she felt it was her fault for being jealous, and for not hugging her before she left for the hospital.

Hearing these things, I was unable to cope any longer. My decision was made. The time was now. I drove to a place where I felt no one could find me. As I looked down from the steep sea cliff, I was ready to jump. Death could be no worse than living, I believed. I was at the lowest part of my life and completely withdrawn. There was nothing left for me to give or feel. It was the hardest struggle to just stay alive. Taking my life would help me escape and eliminate my suffering.

In that premeditated moment, the distraction from the ring of my cell phone forced me to pause. Hearing my cousin Parcy's voice on the other end was a sign from God. I realized the ringing was noise from the outside world forcing me to quiet the noise within myself. This simple sound of a ringtone stopped me from joining Mayra in death.

Every single day I still mourn her. Nothing will bring my younger daughter back. That is the most difficult part. Mayra, who loved to dress in pink and pretend to be a princess, was gone. Even after nine years, the grief I feel is still raw and very overwhelming.

It took time, but I learned to take my greatest pain and make it a blessing to others. I realized that my hardship and grief could help other people through theirs.

A few months after Mayra's death, I met a young girl named Ameyrane, who was suffering from Lupus. She reminded me of my sweet Mayra. I understood what her mother was feeling, and knew that I had to help. Using my own money and my previous experience, I wanted to guide her through the difficulties and messiness of our underfunded and disorganized healthcare system. It was also necessary to help her financially, in addition to finding out more about her child's medical condition. That same help had been missing for me. After that, I began supporting other local families whose children were also dying. This decision provided relief from my own grief and a way to comfort others.

One month before the one-year anniversary of Mayra's death, I was fortunate to begin working for a family from the United States who had three polite children, and a dog named Gunner. They had built a beachfront home in Mexico and needed caretakers. The job requirements were straightforward: Take charge of the daily duties around the house, and look after the property in their absence. Although the husband seemed serious and all business, the wife was very nice. I was ready for a change. I had been praying to find joy among all the pain. This began a new chapter for Ruben and Jessie and me.

The idea of starting a foundation for children was always a thought I had after my child's death. My new employers, especially the serious and selfless husband, were instrumental in helping make my vision a reality. He guided me through the steps of building an established charitable institution, such as filing for tax-exempt status and other legal matters, and of course, helping financially with the initial funding. *Fundación Sonrisas De Carita de Ángel* came to life, and little by little, so did I. As the name says, "An Angel Is Smiling." Yes, that is my Mayra. It took time, but I learned to take my pain and offer it as a blessing to others in need.

This foundation continues to heal my sore heart. Each situation for each family is different. We offer a variety of services, such as providing transportation for treatments, and paying for blood work. We also have covered the costs of nutrition items like PediaSure, and fruity kid yogurts that

Mayra always wanted to eat, but we could never afford. It feels so reassuring to support other children who battle with cancer. The foundation also provides information for parents so they can have a better understanding of the disease their child is struggling with. Sonrisas De Carita de Ángel will continue to support the smiles of other children with cancer in memory of our little Mayrita.

On the eighth anniversary of Mayra's death, I took my oldest daughter to the spot on the cliff where my pain, loss of direction, and deep depression had forced me to contemplate suicide. As Jessie and I looked down from the vertical sea cliff into the greenish-blue clear water full of colorful swimming fish and spiny sea urchins, we commemorated our much-loved Mayra, and the joy of persevering.

Now the sun is shining again through the murkiness, and I thank God. Healing is delicate. It cannot be bought. It cannot be rushed. It cannot be forced. It is different for everyone. I had to allow myself time, first to grieve and then to deal with the pain, ultimately accepting what I cannot change.

I will leave you with a *chistoso* (humorous) story. Two years ago, on my birthday, Ruben was cooking dinner. I will never forget the aroma of stinky goat meat simmering on the stove. It instantly made me feel sick, but forced me to smile at the same time. This was my first clue that I was pregnant again, and it meant my nausea was not caused from the usual pungent smell of that poor animal.

One can never replace a child. Mayra will always be my little angel. The sting of her death will never fade. Ruben and I had struggled to conceive for over four years. I gave up trying, keeping faith in God, and trusting Him to decide whether having another baby was supposed to happen. Having another child is a continued form of healing for me in learning daily to cope with the loss of one angel, while preparing me for the task of raising one more.

God blessed me with my precious Dylan who was born on May 22, 2015, the same month Mayra had been diagnosed with cancer. He is an energetic, strong-willed toddler like Mayra was, and shares a love of iguana tamales with her as well. He loves to breakdance and is full of energy. When he contorts his little, bony arms and legs to create different body movements, my heart soars once again.

I will forever carry in my heart a happy memory. One day after Mayra died, Ruben and I were inside a store and a butterfly landed on his shoulder, three separate times. This gave me comfort and joy. One of my Bible verses talks about the flower dying, but the seed continues to produce fruit for others to enjoy. For me, that beautiful butterfly softly touching Ruben's shoulder was a miracle. It symbolized transformation, representing my Mayra telling me, "All is well."

My world is no longer dark. It is warm, bright. I am fully participating in my life now. I am excited to watch Jessie and Dylan every day. I work hard for my family, and will continue to build my foundation. Ruben recently told me how much he respects me and how proud he is of me. It is nice to have his support considering all that has happened. This was a great compliment, even though he went on to say, "And I love your strong character, but please do not use it on me!"

Chapter Two

Madaline

I have been smitten with this lovely lady for over thirteen years. When she arrived on my doorstep bearing her infamous Heath Bar cake to welcome my family to the neighborhood, I knew we would be friends for a long time. Over the years, we often got together for chats in her bright, airy living room. Today, I take my favorite seat on her striped blue loveseat. Madaline is directly to my left, elegantly erect in a matching blue high-backed chair. The vaulted ceilings and large picture window create a beautiful and pleasantly bright space. I take a minute to admire the African violets along the windowsill, along with the potted orchids bending artfully on her kitchen table.

Our conversations during our long alliance have reminded me that optimism and fortitude are rare and precious personality traits. I relish the time that I have spent with Madaline, and I am grateful for the many stories she has shared with me. Right now I notice she is wearing her classic Rich and Rose Estee Lauder lipstick, as well as her favorite sapphire blue cashmere sweater. I smile and suddenly realize how much I am going to miss seeing her. Our meeting today is bittersweet, since she will be moving to Oregon with her family in a few weeks; my time with her is running short.

Madaline has graced this world with her sunshine and charm for ninety-three years now. From her beginnings as a young immigrant from Germany, she has lived a charmed life filled with love and steadfast determination. Despite losing her best friend and husband of fifty-three years, she continues on her life's journey fueled by courage and generosity. She epitomizes Betty Freidan's premise that aging is not lost youth, but a new stage of opportunity. I am lucky to have her in my life.

As she sips the Starbucks latte that my son has brought for her, I'm struck, as I always am, by the poise and peace that emanate from deep inside this remarkable woman. She exudes elegance in everything she does. And, like the happy blossoms that fill her living room, she doesn't just survive—she thrives!

I feel so blessed that my mother and father had the foresight to come to the United States once Hitler started moving up the ranks, knowing that no good would come of it. Otherwise where would I be?

I was born February 27, 1925. I spent the first five years of my life in an old farmhouse in Edewecht, Germany. I remember a very long and large oak beam running through the length of our thatch-roofed home. I was often scolded for eating too many hazelnuts from our trees, and picking blooms off the flower borders. I don't know if I actually recall my father twirling me between his outstretched arms while holding my hands, or if my mother just told me about it so often that I feel like I remember it myself. At any rate, this is one of the few memories I have of my father.

He came to America ahead of us in May 1930 on the ship *Bremen*. Father headed to California where he stayed with a distant cousin whom we called Uncle Fred, a single man who traveled a lot. He sponsored my father while he gained his citizenship. He also helped him find construction-type jobs here and there. My father had been a master builder back home.

A few months later, my mother Wilhelmina and I crossed the ocean, too. Due to the severe storms, it took us eighteen days instead of the usual thirteen. During the voyage, I remember accidentally dropping my Chinese checkers set. When the pea-sized marbles rolled everywhere, our fellow passengers helped me collect them. From Ellis Island, mother and I took a train to the West Coast. Since we did not speak English, our destination papers were pinned to our lapels.

Six months after we arrived in America, father died suddenly of a heart attack; he was only thirty-three. I believe his death was hastened by gas poisoning from his fighting in World War I. Although mother never talked about it, it had to have been a terrifying time for her. She did not speak any English, had very little money, and also had to care for a five-year-old.

In her late teens, my mother had attended six months of cooking school. In Germany, farmers often sent their girls away to learn how to cook so that when they returned home they could take on culinary duties for the family. Mother was a superior cook and baker, always knowing when things tasted just right. Her angel food cake was amazingly light and layered beautifully with fresh whipped cream and sweet strawberries. Her cheesecake was rich and luscious. People were always in awe of her talents in the kitchen. I was, too.

After father died, Uncle Fred offered my mother a job as a cook in the lunchroom he operated out of his home. He told her that every once in a while a wealthy man stopped by for coffee and he might be looking for someone to cook for him full time.

Uncle Fred owned a lot of land. He had a modest house located at the horseshoe curve of Moody Road in Los Altos, California, right before the steep grade leading to the farms and ranches. Countless people stopped by for a sandwich or beverage after mother started working for him there. But it ended up being her deep-fried chicken and syrup cookies that afforded us the opportunity that changed our lives.

Milton Haas, the wealthy gentleman whom Uncle Fred had told my mother about, lived a few miles down the road. Sure enough, her brief stint in the lunchroom tingled his taste buds. He hired mother immediately. We moved into his place, and she began working as the family's personal chef, with various other responsibilities including general housekeeping, laundering, and shopping. Mother even oversaw the seven gardeners, hiring and firing them as needed.

I was spoiled living on a beautiful 120-acre estate in the Bay Area, with a gracious and generous man treating me like his own daughter. When I was a teenager, Mr. Haas had young women from his girlfriend's clothing store come to the house to model different outfits and jewelry for me. Then I was invited to choose the ones I wanted. I still remember one custom-made periwinkle blue dress with a pleated skirt and the strand of pearls I wore with it. As you can guess, I never missed a Shirley Temple or Sonia Henie movie! These were all normal indulgences for me since my new life included many extravagances, though I always kept with me a special gift from my father: a German leather doll with a porcelain head and arms.

In school, gymnastics was a joy for me. I think somehow the jumping and spinning reminded me of my father twirling me when I was young. At one point, Mr. Haas must have grown tired of watching me hanging from the branches of his trees, because eventually he had a gymnastics bar erected next to the pool so I could practice my acrobatic feats. My best friend, Trudy, and I used to perform duets for Mr. Haas and his guests during the fancy luncheons he hosted.

One day three orange cats wandered onto the property; I quickly claimed them as my own. Trudy and I amused ourselves for hours in the backyard building houses out of cardboard for the cats. Mr. Haas also had two dogs. One was a 180-pound Irish wolfhound, and the other was Jerry, my favorite, an all-white shepherd with rust spots. Smokey was the fluffy black and grey Persian cat who woke me up every morning for school.

Although he pampered me, Mr. Haas also felt strongly about my education. He always tested me on my spelling. Mother continually stressed the importance of education as well. I remember her telling me, "Never get upset if you get a bad grade. If you studied, I will never scold you."

Life was wonderful growing up, and this inspired me to have my own ambitions and aspirations. I remember in the third grade, a bunch of us girls were chattering about our futures and all the things we were going to do. I had three desires: to attend Stanford University; to marry a tall, dark and handsome man who could make a lot of money; and go to Hawaii.

After graduating high school, I attended San Jose State my freshman year and worked at a real estate office on Saturdays. I was afraid to take the Stanford entrance exam; I needed time to finally muster up the courage. I passed and entered Stanford as a sophomore, one of only thirty females accepted in 1944!

WWII was taking place, and many of the boys at Stanford were in the R.O.T.C. I remember one time a group of us were talking together in the quad, sharing where we were from. I told the truth to everyone that I was born in Germany. It never crossed my mind not to be honest. One young R.O.T.C. man said, "You're a Nazi!" I was shocked and humiliated. Though I was an immigrant to this country, I had never thought of myself as different. And I had never been treated like I was an outsider! Until that day, I had not experienced the stigmas and prejudices certain people had about immigrants. His comment upset me for many years. I finally went to a therapist to help rid myself of this sense of inferiority.

After I turned twenty-one, I automatically became a United States citizen. I proudly graduated from Stanford in 1947 with a degree in art history. Originally, I was a pre-architecture major, yet taking trigonometry twice made me reconsider that course of study. I thoroughly enjoyed the art classes, especially learning how to work with watercolor and charcoal. It felt satisfying to accomplish one of my three goals!

After graduation, I started working full time at Floyd Lowe Realty where I worked three years before. One day a tall, clean-cut guy swaggered in, attempting to drum up commerce and connections for a title company he managed. Little did I know, but Bob Stratton's interests shifted my way—and it ended up being romantic business that he found that day!

After our first date, he took both my hands and told me, "Such a fun evening we've had; let's do it more often." Nothing more, not even a kiss on the cheek, yet I was smitten with this chivalrous man and his piercing blue eyes. We started seeing each other almost every day.

Bob and I were married in the incredibly beautiful Stanford Memorial Chapel. A few weeks before our wedding we were asked to be contestants on a television show called *Betty Wing's Your Hope Chest*. It was similar to *The Newlywed Game* that was around in the late '60s. Three couples had to answer general life questions about each other. We won the grand prize: a $250 wedding cake, along with a week at Sierra Sky Ranch outside Yosemite National Park!

I was madly in love with my tall, dark and handsome husband. His gentleness and kind spirit stole my heart. And he had such a sharp sense of humor! Our marriage created a wave of fifty-three wondrous years together. We laughed and gardened and raised our only son, Randy. We also had the chance to visit Hawaii several times. Indeed, I had accomplished everything on my adolescent wish list.

My loving husband understood that marrying me was a package deal—he knew my mother would be living with us from day one. However, he never questioned me or made me feel guilty about it; he was a true gentleman. She lived with us until her death in 1984, at 100, plus one week, crediting her longevity to taking two teaspoons of honey a day.

When mother died, my darling husband gently joked, "No more stinky traditional German kale dishes!" Bob would eat her mixture of kale, rolled oats, and onion that mother made—the fragrance always made him turn up his nose, but he ate it. So at fifty-nine with mother gone, I had to start learning how to cook! I began watching Martha Stewart religiously. My mother never allowed anyone in the kitchen with her, and Martha's mother would often join her on the show. This dichotomy always brought a smile to my face.

I was seventy-eight when my husband, the love of my life, passed away. I found myself all alone for the first time in my life. I was devastated. My granddaughter Lauren stayed with me for two weeks after his death to help me acclimate, since I was so overwhelmed by the loss. Tony, our pure white Samoyed dog, slept every night with me on Bob's side of the bed. When he was alive, Tony had slept on the floor beside Bob. Dogs are much smarter than we ever give them credit for.

Being alone was terrifying. Many times I would cry and ask God to bring mother and Bob back. I ate cottage cheese for lunch and boiled eggs for dinner. I couldn't stand the silent house. I always had the television or radio on. Listening to classical music programs and André Rieu's waltz-like melodies made me think of Bob. That soothed me. Then I wondered how mother managed after father died? Did she feel the same way? I never asked her.

Bob had handled all our finances and paperwork. All the computer passwords were in his desk, but I was not certain what they applied to and how to use them. I had to figure out everyday tasks that I had never done before. Nevertheless, persistence got me through. What choice did I have? Thankfully, God gave me courage to face each new day, in addition to wonderful friends who offered their support.

During that transition time, I tried to keep very busy. I baked cheesecakes for church auctions, using mother's recipe, of course! I also participated in the Stephen Ministry program, offering comfort and help to people dealing with death, chronic illness, or even financial troubles. I like to extend support and hope to others, because that's what Mr. Haas did for me and mother. I also made floral arrangements for the Pleasant Valley Hospital where I volunteered at the reception desk twice a week greeting and guiding visitors, making them feel at ease. In fact, the hospital just recognized me for over thirteen years of service!

I have been a widow, still living in my lovely home for fourteen years now. I used to go upstairs to sit in Bob's office with its rich wood built-ins, overlooking my now overgrown garden. I would gaze down at the discolored brass tracks that my enthusiast husband assembled for his German trains that used to circle through my Love and Peace tea rose bushes in the backyard. Unfortunately, I can no longer make it up those stairs, let alone get into the garden to trim that stephanotis vine.

Aging alone is not fun. My main ailment is chronic pain from degenerative arthritis, which has attached itself to my back. Sometimes I can hardly stand the discomfort and I have to use a walker, yet I recognize my decline is minor compared to many others. I never heard my parents grumble, so neither will I. Rebuilding my life without Bob and mother, the cornerstones of my foundation, was hard. But I took on my new normal with a smile. I truly believe both of them are looking down at me from heaven, proud and amazed.

I am now looking forward to living in Oregon with my son, Randy, and daughter-in-law, Carol, who are building me a lovely little granny flat on their property. I will be able to share the next years with my much-loved grandchildren Lauren and Justin, and my great-grandchildren Braelynn, Jackson and Sophie. We will be four generations living under one roof. How rare is that!

I am excited to participate in family dinners and birthdays together. Little Sophie loves when I read her stories about the little pig, and the man with a funny hat. Once I get settled, I may go to the local hospital and ask if they need a volunteer. I hope they do not ask my age, though! At ninety-three, I am very blessed to have the life I do.

Chapter Three

Brigitte

When Brigitte and I first spoke on the phone, I instantly felt an enormous dose of warmth through the receiver. During our twenty-minute conversation, she offered me a brief snapshot of her life. That glimpse was intriguing enough for me to book a flight and hop on a plane to Austin, Texas a few weeks later. I was eager to get to know this strong but gentle woman, who experienced a life-changing accident at the age of twenty-nine that had a powerful effect on her in unexpected ways.

She picked me up at my adult version of a modern treehouse hotel and we drove a short distance to Uchi, a sushi restaurant near a trendy area in Austin. Although the popular eatery was full of activity, our first face-to-face time was just as stimulating as our phone conversation. We spoke casually and shared a few candid stories about common interests (traveling) and delights (participating in alternative healing arts). I was extremely impressed by how the wait staff at Uchi knew her by name and expressed regret for no longer having her favorite pitchfork rolls on the menu.

After dinner, relaxing in her five-hundred-square-foot art studio adjacent to her home, we moved from chitchat to deeper dialogue. Sipping licorice tea, Brigitte beamed as she reminisced about her son, Luke, now twenty-four, who would design sculptures on the oversized drawing table in the corner. When he was just three, she recalled providing him with pliable oven-bake clay, Sculpey, so it wouldn't dry out while he shaped two-dimensional faces.

I was repeatedly distracted from our conversation by the magnetism of her workspace. Various sizes of dreamy oil paintings, full of color and life, hung at different heights on all four walls. Next to a large easel holding a portrait in progress, jars jammed full of paintbrushes sat on a turquoise metal cart with wheels. Alongside the cart was an oversized wooden color palette stained with puddles of paint. It was the classic vision of an artist's studio—a lotus in full bloom of creativity, similar to the vibrant flowers and trees outside her window.

As Brigitte began to articulate her life story, every word seemed graceful and carefully chosen. She embodies a sense of peace and graciousness. I could not help but be in awe of someone who understands art and its restorative benefits. Over the years, using her creative expressions in many shapes and forms, Brigitte healed herself, while opening regenerative pathways to greater overall wellness in her life.

Life is packed full of uncontrollable events. In many situations, the only thing we can control is the attitude we hold when we *choose to respond to adversity. Brigitte is a living example of the most useful way to barter with reality. A true Sagittarius, she is a seeker of truth. When the answers do not immediately arrive, she never allows circumstances to steal her joy and brightness, showing how battles are won from the inside.*

It was a hot and muggy Fourth of July in 1986. I was walking with my husband, Todd, and a group of friends in Tribeca, a neighborhood in Lower Manhattan. At the time, that district was much less crowded than it is now. We lived on Reade Street and West Broadway in a great loft on the sixth floor, without an elevator. Lacking an intercom in the building as well, when friends visited us, we would put the keys in a rolled-up sock and throw it out the window to their waiting hands in the street. I still remember those wide warehouse windows and weathered wood floors.

Todd and I had just finished viewing an interactive, outdoor exhibition space where eight of us had spent two hours admiring countless cutting-edge architectural pieces. The giant vertical sand sculptures amazed me, while several oversized spools of carefully arranged electrical wire brought out the child in me; I was just aching to climb up and crawl inside each intricate arrangement.

We were all casually walking back to our place after watching the holiday fireworks, chattering about the art we had seen. Our friend, Bill, had his little two-year-old son on his shoulders. I remember it was so hot that I regretted my decision to wear my favorite straight-legged jeans with embroidered flowers.

Suddenly without warning, something struck me directly in my right eye.

The original cherry bombs were declared illegal in 1966 by the federal government, since these very powerful explosives are not considered consumer fireworks. They contain more than one gram of flash powder. Red in color and approximately one inch in diameter, this firecracker bomb was lit and thrown out of a window from the high-rise apartment building we were walking past. With its fuse ignited, it hit the ground and then bounced up into my face.

Unsure of what had hit me, I immediately put my hand to my right eye. I was acutely aware of a soothing sensation of warmth. Whatever I was experiencing actually felt good; a deep warmness was permeating my entire being. I had a sense that arms were enfolding me. Although it was evident that neither my husband nor my friends were embracing me, "something" was. I do not recall being in pain; it was a conscious impression of the presence of love encircling me with a total quality of belonging.

I struggle to describe the reassurance and calm I felt at that precise moment. I do remember being objectively coherent, not screaming in agony. Whatever was happening, the intensity of emotion I felt exceeded any normal experience I had ever had—it was much, much bigger. The best way I can express it would be that I was the recipient of an intense experience of compassion and deep affection—a type of divine love enveloped my *being*.

I experienced a sudden illumination, struck by grace and clarity. In Japanese, *satori* means enlightenment, or quite literally "a kick in the eye." In the Zen Buddhist tradition, satori refers to the experience of seeing into one's true nature. Indeed, the silent situation I was experiencing at that moment would send me on a lifelong search for the source of this love.

I was rushed to Bellevue Hospital in an ambulance. My eye socket had been torn open from above the eyebrow to just below my lower eyelid. I vaguely recall the paramedics attempting to hold my eyeball in its socket during the transfer. Up until my arrival at the hospital, I do not remember taking any medications to reduce my pain, since I was not experiencing any distress.

That first hospital stay lasted more than a week. My retina had been pulled off with the impact of the cherry bomb and had to be reattached. Over the next few weeks, and then into months, I had three more operations. Each one was an attempt to reattach the retina, which kept being pulled off by scar tissue as it healed. Both of my eyes were bandaged to keep my pupils evenly dilated.

While I was healing, I would listen to classical music at the hospital, reflecting back over my twenty-nine years. Colors, shapes, forms in space and textures—all these elements of art throughout my life became a prominent memory.

I was born in Morocco in 1956, the year of independence from France. My fond memories of Casablanca have always been the intense colors, the food and the sea. Decorative doorways in varying shades of blue, some of them wooden, distressed and cracked, stir up an intensity of emotion, as do the vibrant red peppers drying on the roof in the sun for days. I recalled going back to visit my grandparents when I was younger and tasting *dafina*, a slow-cooked layered stew made with wheat, chickpeas, pumpkin, beef and chicken (bones included). The smoothness of the majestic Moroccan dresses, the *kaftans* with their coherent patterns and lustrous colors, still bring cheerfulness to my heart.

We moved to Paris when I was just a year old. When I think of that enchanting city, I see my mother standing on the black wrought iron Juliet balcony of our apartment on *Rue de Moscou* waving to my brother and me as we walked to school. Our school building, cream in color with square stacked glass bricks arranged in art deco style, was across the street from our apartment. The park nearby was my preferred place to be, especially when the marionette *(guignol)* show was performing. Strings on my limbs would have been the only way I would perform in front of people. The thought of being on stage terrified me; I could relate to the puppets hanging in limbo on the back of the makeshift platform.

My father, a very ambitious businessman was offered a position as CEO of an export company in the United States. At six, moving from France to the USA and living on Grace Avenue in Great Neck, Long Island was a profound culture shock for me. French, my first language, is what we spoke at home. Thank goodness it did not take me long to understand English words and form the sounds to speak it. On the other hand, the social and emotional learning in our new country was more challenging for me.

American kids were eating TV dinners in front of the television, while I was eating multiple courses in our formal dining room with cloth napkins. Lamb brains in an omelet, and a cheese course instead of cookies for dessert were customary for our family. To make matters worse, my mother would not allow me to dress in jeans and tennis shoes, but outfitted me in a dark green wool cape over my dress to wear to school.

As a teenager, I spent many days in my room gazing at my sheer silk cobalt blue curtains from Morocco, wondering how life would have been different growing up there instead. The repeated white-on-white arabesques invited my mind to meander. I learned to be an observer; people would say I was extremely introverted. This disposition continued throughout my teenage years, making it challenging for me to fit in; I often felt like an outcast.

From ages six to sixteen, I would spend summers in France or Morocco. Although I loved going abroad, it made it even harder for me to fit in back in New York. I felt like I didn't belong anyplace; I seemed to be in a continuous transitional state, which to a young person was problematic, to say the least.

After high school, I attended Cornell University for two-and-a-half years in upstate New York. The campus was gorgeous; the red brick buildings were covered with bright green ivy. Located on 2,300 acres of green rolling hills above Lake Cayuga, it was a paradise. This is where I began my degree in architecture, before switching to fine arts.

It is also where I met my first husband. He was visiting a friend who lived in the apartment above me. Todd was five years older than me, working as an architect designing large-scale tension structures. I liked his bad boy persona and creative side, not to mention his thrill-seeking ways. We would often climb the bridges around Manhattan: the Brooklyn, the George Washington, and Verrazano. We were fiery, reckless and in love.

After meeting Todd in my third year at Cornell, we moved into lower Manhattan together; I transferred to the New York Studio School. This historical landmark with its pink and grey exterior is located in Manhattan on 8th Street in a stately looking building with an eagle above the entryway. While I studied there, they taught art in a way that felt Old World, very classical. I was under the watchful eye of Leland Bell and Paul Resika, two much-loved American painters. It was a unique experience to spend half the day drawing and the other half painting, both still life compositions and working with live models. My life was art!

Todd and I were living in a warehouse loft off Bowery on Rivington Street. I remember rescuing Rico, a mutt at the subway station, who was standing, cold and alone, looking for love; I could not resist. Rico and I shared similar spirits and were inseparable for many years. My furry friend and I then returned to Cornell where I finished my degree, earning a BFA. Todd and I married at City Hall in July 1979.

In my twenties now, I was beginning to not feel as marginal as I had felt growing up. In truth, I started to feel a bit

wild, living the high life of an artist in NYC, clubbing, partying, experimenting with designer drugs, dressing up (think
Madonna in the '80s), and frequenting places like the Mud
Club, CBGB's, and Area, another nightclub that changed
locations and themes repeatedly. It was definitely a fertile time
for artists of all fields in Manhattan.

I felt very lucky when I started working as a color mixer
at Larry B. Wright Art Production, a silkscreen fine art print
studio in the heart of Little Italy. The *Salumeria,* an Italian
deli across the street from the silkscreen shop, had the most
amazing hero sandwiches, with the best Italian bread. The
print studio did one series for Andy Warhol, his Howdy Doody
reproductions. After working there for two years, I decided
to enroll for my master's degree at Parsons School of Design.
During the second year of my master's program, I went abroad
to Florence at the Studio Arts Center International to study
the fresco painting technique. Todd and I were living in the
loft in Tribeca by that time.

When the bandages were finally removed from my eyes,
I realized my inner critic had become more compassionate.
I was a painter, with no recourse but to return to my easel
with only one functioning eye. Consequently, painting for
me naturally became about sensation, no longer simply visual
information. I began to approach color, form and light with a
more expanded feeling of freedom.

Life was becoming a journey of finding the source of the
divine acceptance I had experienced that fateful day. The
accident the summer of 1986 brought clarity to my relationship with Todd as well. I realized I was living *through* him,

never having a sense of my own self. Feeling too much like his Madame Matisse, I wanted my purpose now. I do believe, however, all artists need encouragement and even reverence from their partners. I certainly idolized Todd, yet at this moment in my life I wanted someone to take care of me and support my art. We went our separate ways after ten years of being together.

Gratefully, my parents lived near us on 70th Street, between 2nd and 3rd Avenue, a neighborhood surrounded by magnolia and dogwood trees. I will never forget the warm cherry wood and green marble in the lobby of their apartment. Thank goodness they lived close by and were available to nurse me back to health. During each hospital stay, I remember listening to recordings of opera, while eating celery, endives and cucumbers, drinking Evian water and Orangina.

Alone now, I wanted to deepen my understanding of my heightened sense of awareness. Like a sixth sense, I started paying attention to the signs and opportunities around me, becoming more mindful and open. I began my exploration into yoga, thanks to my father who gave me his VHS yoga tapes, telling me he found them useful during his cancer recovery. One of my female friends, Hank, suggested I try the Japanese martial art called *Aikido* when she saw me practicing yoga. I met my second husband Kim, an apprentice to the Aikido Master Imaizumi at the *dojo*. Practicing Aikido allowed me to be aware of the energy around me, which was very beneficial, considering my limited vision.

Kim also introduced me to Integral Yoga. I started taking classes in the pink brick building on 13th Street. It felt like being inside a beating heart tucked within a grey concrete jungle. Nine months after my accident, I visited Yogaville, an ashram in Virginia. Meditating in the Lotus Shrine was a deeply mystical experience for me. I also participated in a silent retreat, which turned out to be a cathartic release of tears and a turning point for me.

My guru, His Holiness Sri Swami Satchidananda, one of the most revered yoga masters of our time and founder of Integral Yoga, was at the ashram when I was there. I admit that he was the main catalyst to my spiritual growth. After my time in retreat, reentering the world of sound, I remember being in awe of everything, as if I was riding a pink cloud of love. This was a similar experience to when I lost my sight in one eye.

In April 1987, I traveled alone for ten months across the country in a yellow VW van I named Honey. I found this yellow beauty in the classifieds and had a very strong inner knowing that this trip was what I needed to do. It turned out to be an empowering experience for me. While listening to Ray Charles and Muddy Waters on my cassette player cruising with Honey throughout the West, I was brought face-to-face with my fears, over and over again. Yet through it all, I felt a sense of Divine protection and love.

I eventually made my way to Texas where Kim joined me; then we traveled together through Mexico. We lived together for a short time in Woodstock, NY. One year later we moved to Austin, and we have been here ever since.

When I think back to that instant warmth that flooded my body over thirty years ago on the street, I continue to have an insatiable thirst for transcendence. Apart from calling it divine intervention, I have spent a lifetime trying to satisfy that yearning. I am always reminded to not look outside, but inside myself to discover that place where every fiber of my being felt fully alive. Yoga remains my number one way to Source. It's a continual inward spiraling journey, for sure!

When my eyes were bandaged, I only saw the shadow side. Yet I did not ever want my world to be made solely of shades of grey or nothingness, but of colors and textures. I felt, and still feel, a sense of liberation in splattering colors on a canvas. Painting allows me to produce a million different impressions for the eye. I love color as a way to express myself emotionally. I enjoy pushing the edges of my truth, as I continue to dive more deeply into that heavenly love within myself.

Chapter Four

Lauren

What do you think about when you hear the word "beautiful" as it refers to a woman? Our reflections in the mirror are often distorted by society's constructs of beauty. Movies, magazines, and social media bombard us with flawless yet constantly shifting images, which can be disheartening even to the most confident of us. We must continually remind ourselves that no matter what we look like, we are beautiful.

Lauren is a spirited sixteen-year-old with the emotional maturity of a woman many times her age. With a short, spunky hairstyle that matches her persona, she reminds me that we are as beautiful as we allow ourselves to be. Her bright, airy bedroom reflects who she is as an individual. Lauren's favorite scented candle, Volcano from Anthropologie, wafted the scent of tropical fruit, while the dancing flame mimicked our energetic exchange.

Sitting under the twinkling lights that adorn her white canopy bed, we compared notes over some of our similar people-pleasing tendencies, and shared acute anxiety triggers. She revealed her many phases of depression to me, as well as her past struggles with self-harm, including the release it offered when no one seemed to understand the emptiness she was feeling inside.

Throughout the leisurely afternoon we spent together, Izzy, Lauren's sweet Golden Retriever, listened and snorted a few times at pivotal points in our conversation. Izzy clearly had something to say about the importance of being a non-conformist to stereotypical beauty standards. Or she may have just wanted a bit more of the Brie and red grapes we were snacking on.

Lauren bravely endeavors to create awareness of the psychological disorders that she has struggled with in her life. In 2014, shortly before entering a treatment center, she started her own YouTube channel under the username Lolochic. Three years and over ninety videos later, she has 4,000 subscribers and over 400,000 total views. With everything from DIYs to fun challenges, beauty tutorials to body positivity messages, this young warrior woman is taking her vulnerability and know-how and presenting it worldwide to women of all ages needing support. I am equally amazed that she handles all the script writing, music, and editing herself!

We can't heal what we never reveal. Lauren is a living example of this. Her story won't be everyone's story, but it sheds light on the way we ascribe meaning to illness. So without further ado, meet Lolochic.

Hello lovelies! Lolochic here. You guys are absolutely amazing! Each and every one of you viewers inspire me every day.

In today's video, I want to share something a bit more personal. I'm a big fan of vulnerability, and I strongly believe in speaking about my struggles with the hope of helping and supporting others in their difficulties and challenges. As someone in the midst of ongoing conflict with her body image and mental health, self-love is something very dear and near to my heart. I truly believe that to be present and selfless, we have to love and accept ourselves as we are right now.

I was diagnosed with anorexia, an eating disorder, when I was thirteen. It started around the time I turned ten, and lasted for three-and-a-half years. During that time, I felt too anxious to put food in my mouth, chew it, and swallow it. There was always a knot in my stomach, and I would immediately become nauseous at the idea of having to eat. Although the anxiety I was experiencing was not rooted in food itself, it evolved into body perception issues, along with a fear of actually having to eat anything.

A small circle of my girlfriends at school were trying to be thin and gorgeous like Candice Swanepoel. In case you don't know, she is a top model and a Victoria's Secret Angel, with legs longer than my whole body! After studying pictures of her and knowing I wanted to emulate her in every way, I told my family, "I'm giving up bread forever!"

I would typically only eat simple things like yogurt and fruit. That was the extent of my comfort zone, especially at school. On Pizza Fridays, it was extremely hard. Every week

I felt like I was forced to have pizza that day, and dreaded it as soon as I opened my eyes in the morning. It would be just *me* versus the *pizza*. Most of the time, there could have been things going on in the background in the lunchroom, or a big group of people around me socializing, but all I could focus on was the *pizza*. My throat would feel like it was closing up, which by the way, is called restriction. My hands would shake, and I would start to get nauseous. My body would be freaking out just *looking* at a piece of pizza.

To be honest, any time I was eating in front of people, especially boys, I was scared. It was a huge deal for me in eighth grade when I finally picked up a slice of pizza in front of a boy and took a bite. Even though everyone around me at the table was enjoying eating, and I desperately wanted to be a part of the crowd, I just couldn't make myself put food in my mouth. And since I could not be in that moment with them by eating something, I would then remove myself from conversations and get super quiet and withdrawn.

During those years, I also had a tendency to get caught up in a negative mindset. I would look in the mirror and fixate on things that I specifically didn't like about myself—like how my butt was way on the curvy side. Oh, did I mention my stretch marks and the cellulite? The image I saw was not the "me" I wanted to be. Especially the cellulite.

I struggled constantly with self-love and positivity during those years. I still do. Maybe everyone does, I don't know. I have battled severe depression and anxiety for nearly four years, including bouts of self-harm—but for only a couple of months after treatment. I was frustrated because I had put so much work into my eating to then cope with my emptiness in another way. For me, cutting myself became a way of validating the emotions I was experiencing. It wasn't really to show others that I was hurting; it was more to prove to myself that my pain was real. It didn't make sense to me to be so miserable without a clear reason—cutting gave me a physical representation of my emotional pain.

Okay, this may be getting heavy for you viewers, but *seriously,* it's important.

Then two months before my fourteenth birthday, I entered a treatment center to help me with my extreme emotions, attitudes, and behaviors surrounding my weight and food. This was one of the hardest things I have done in my life! It took a ton of work and a few months of missing school, but I finally realized I had the power to influence my mind and body when everything around me felt frantic.

My therapist, Lissa, is one of my favorite people in the entire world. She told me once, "Stop sitting in your own shit." This really stuck in my mind! The therapists, staff, and other patients at the facility never made me feel like I was sick. The other girls and I bonded over our personal struggles, while sipping mint tea out of the cutest little teacups. We formed a real sisterhood in that charming yellow house. My motto from that time on became, *"I can do hard things!"*

In November 2016, about eighteen months after I left the treatment center, a family friend gave birth to a baby boy named Graham. This young fellow has the most beautiful blue eyes! I was still struggling with my old habit patterns, yet he had a huge impact on my life. The first time I held him and felt his little hand grab onto my finger, I promised myself I would live as a positive example for him. This really helped me to stop cutting.

I understand now how much my mental health and mindset really affect what I do. It is not easy to stay positive every single day. *Trust me!* It is not easy at all! I guess I thought recovery meant I would not struggle in the same way ever again, and that I would always be happy. I thought I had paid my debts of pain and I was finally in the clear.

I soon learned that *was not true!*

Of course, I still have negative thoughts about myself! Learning to cope with my anxiety does not mean I don't battle with it on a daily basis. Improving my body image does not mean that sometimes I don't break down in tears because of how I see myself in the mirror. My old negative habits still arise for me.

It has also taken time for me to realize that accepting help in different forms isn't being weak—it's me being strong! I take *Zoloft,* an antidepressant, together with a mood stabilizer. I also use a personalized homeopathic remedy, *causticum*—a little white bead that melts under my tongue. I think it's from some type of flower. I know there can be a stigma attached to taking medication for mental health issues, but I've finally managed to let go of that shame. I wish all pills were the shape and flavor of Gummy Bear vitamins, but oh well!

Healing is never a straight path. There are highs and lows, twists and turns from the very start—and there really is no end. Staying positive, especially during hard times, is not easy. Occasionally, I feel like a living, breathing burden, who negatively affects everyone around me. I know it will take time to fully understand how sometimes I can feel so unloved and unworthy of love when I have people telling me the opposite of that every day.

But deep down, I know I am loved and wanted, and that I have value. And it is super comforting to know that now I can be totally open with my friends, family or therapist about what is going on for me, whether I feel crazy or just fine. I can reach out to them for help and support during those tough times, especially when I find it difficult to quell the negative voices in my head.

With prayer, along with all my tools from therapy, and an awesome support system, I am able to pull myself out of the depths of self-hatred and despair. When the voices start up, I can remind myself, this is not you, Lauren. This is not who you are or who you want to be. Ignore the voices, Lauren!

When my phases of depression or panic flare up, I can choose to really immerse myself in my hobbies to distract my negative thoughts, and keep calm and centered. Two of my favorite "go-to's" are working on videos for my YouTube channel and embroidery. I learned how to embroider sitting on my grandmother's lap when I was little. I've recently made a bunny and elephant blankie for Graham. And I'm planning to sell a few of my other designs online through Etsy.

In March 2017, I celebrated the two-year anniversary of my treatment by running a half-marathon! That's right. *I ran a half-marathon!* Those of you who know me understand how crazy that sounds.

Never, ever did I think I would or could run a half-marathon race. It really gave me a sense of accomplishment and purpose, boosting my self-esteem to unknown heights. I ran with Team World Vision, raising money to help provide clean water for the kids and communities in Africa.

Truly, I am not ashamed of what I've been through; I'm actually empowered by it! Through all of this, I realize the greatest gift I can give myself is trying my best to embrace my weaknesses, and keep getting stronger to defeat the negative moods. I love myself because I do and have done hard things.

Each day I dig deep to find the courage to continue challenging myself to be the best version of who I am, really connecting with others, and living life with a positive attitude. I am so lucky to have an amazing, caring and loving support team, including my best friend Justin, who is hilarious and makes me laugh extremely hard, and my family (Mom, Dad, Melissa and Jake) who are also pretty cool.

I am learning to let go and face the world, anxiety and all! I am also learning that cellulite is totally normal.

That's all for now! Lovelies, be proud of who you are every day! Thanks for watching and listening. Be back with you soon!

Barbara Jean

Five horses gallop past the Spanish-style equestrian center where I am waiting for Barbara Jean. Gazing through a water-stained window, I admire the rugged terrain and abundant green pastures outside. Both the lady and the location—a 6,000-acre working thoroughbred farm in Ventura County—are hidden jewels. It has been a while since I have seen her, and I am excited to hear how she is doing.

Barbara Jean's endurance rivals that of the horses she trains and adores. I met her a few years ago in a delicatessen near the Del Mar Racetrack. We each enjoyed a bowl of chicken dumpling soup and a Corona Light with a little piece of lime, while she captivated me with audacious accounts of her life. I remember thinking to myself, "This woman is one tough cookie!"

She has had a long, thrilling career as a horsewoman, with plenty of bumps and bruises to show for it. She manages to brush herself off, grab the reins, and courageously put herself back in

the saddle again and again and again. Her continued eagerness
to participate in activities with obvious physical risks, always
offset by an emotional reward, intrigues me. And her resilience,
both physical and emotional, is beyond remarkable.

Sitting in a western-themed apartment on the ranch,
I began to jot down a few notes. The ranch manager stopped by
to inform me Barbara Jean would be a little late. She was dealing
with her "barn of misfits" – twelve horses, two of them her own,
that require a little more understanding than most of the equine
species. Less than fifteen minutes later, the screen door opened
and in she walked, wearing her standard smile and a sterling
silver and turquoise necklace that read, "The best hearts are
the bravest."

George was an old thoroughbred horse, as long as a city block,
which is how my three sisters and I could all fit on his back
together. Sweet George, with the white narrow stripe down
his nose, would let each of us mount him, unfazed. We had
so much fun riding him bareback. As the youngest, I would
always sit nearest his tail and dig my heels into his belly,
causing him to buck. To this day, I am still not entirely sure my
squealing sisters knew I was the one producing this reaction.
I had always been obsessed with horses, but George was the
first one to steal my heart.

All through my childhood years, maybe ages five through
twelve, my friends and I used to barrel race in our backyard

field. When we got tired of being confined, we rode through the neighbor's pastures, jumping over old Cadillac convertibles they had turned into feed wagons. We liked to pretend we were Indians riding bareback, so we used colored fingerpaints to stamp our drippy handprints all over the horses' bodies, making our own tribal war paint patterns. It was delightful!

Sometimes we had "weddings" for the horses. Peaches married Rod; Lucky married Bam Bam. We would make a cake for each couple consisting of warm oats and water in an aluminum container. For a bit of flare, whole carrots stood upright as candles. The horses never failed to delight in their treats.

I remember when I was in third grade, I was supposed to be in bed with the flu. But I snuck out to ride my horse Rod, a calm Chestnut gelding. He was seventeen hands high with a copper-reddish coat. Since one hand equals four inches, he was really tall, especially for an eight-year-old little girl. Grabbing his mane, swinging my heel over his withers and wiggling up his neck was the only way I could get up. I was told not to ride Rod because his feet were too long, which could cause him to trip and fall. Yet feeling invincible, I went anyhow.

Sure enough, while galloping in the field, Rod stumbled and rolled on top of me. As I lay on the ground, I saw the forest through the trees, along with a bright, almost blinding light. I had lost consciousness; a complete sense of calm surrounded me, unlike the reality of the trauma of his 1,450 pounds. When my sister Susie found me and alerted my parents, they called 911, and the ambulance took me to the hospital. I had suffered severe head injuries that kept me in a coma for six weeks. This was my first major injury from the animals I loved.

After my hospital stay, my body and head were still aching, but so was my heart to get back in the saddle. With a black and blue body, and water on my knee, I was back riding Rod! Although it was hard to canter on his back, at least I was reunited with my hoofed friend. The most annoying part was the repercussions of my sisters tattling on me, since I was not supposed to be riding *anything* yet.

My emotional bond with horses deepened when Rod had a horrific accident, cracking his head on a fencepost. As I witnessed blood coming out of his ears and nose, they could not pull me off him. I was devastated. Wherever his next life was taking him, I wanted to go. I knew he was going to die. It was not fair for him to leave me here on Earth alone.

Afterwards, I had frightening dreams that left me at the foot of my parents' bed, upset for days that turned into weeks. Rod and I had a special trust and kinship. I lost my best friend in the world that day. He was a regular good ole' boy with plenty of spunk. I will never forget riding him in parades, dressing him up and braiding his mane to match my own hair.

Less than a year later, my thrifty father found me a free horse named Reyna, who was half-Arabian. Afraid of her own shadow and extremely hyperactive, working with Reyna helped me heal my broken heart. Maybe we both recognized the distress in each other. I trained her daily and she went on to be a successful show-jumping horse. All through my teenage years, my four-legged friends were encouraging me get to know myself better, giving me the courage and freedom to be me.

The day I got my driver's license, I drove down to Mexico alone in our family's gold and white station wagon, pulling an extra-long horse trailer. It was my sixteenth birthday and I was picking up April, a five-year-old dark brown mare with a white star on her face. I had started working at the boarding stables feeding horses, cleaning stalls, and (eventually) giving riding lessons. I saved up my hard-earned money and paid $1,000 for her. She was unbroken and infested with ticks, but she was the best gift a girl could give herself. I was really excited!

Little did I know that after loading April on the trailer, eight men decided to load in as well. The border patrol stopped me and we were detained for half the day. Once cleared to cross the border, we finally made it home. April was happy to have me in her life. She was a pretty little mare who needed some TLC and kind human interactions.

After graduating high school, I decided to go to college for pre-veterinary education at Cal Poly, San Luis Obispo. I also worked at Rio Vista Ranch breaking yearlings. Although that sounds awful to someone not familiar with horses, it just means training a horse to allow a human on its back. One of my classes required me to break a yearling and enter it into the Two-Year-Olds in Training Sale at the Hollywood Park Racetrack. However, I never ended up finishing my degree because of the amazing opportunities I encountered both at the racetrack and at Rio Vista Ranch.

My life changed when I met top trainer Charlie Whittingham. I respected his style of training, since his horses were always happy and content. I remember feeling out of my league, but I wanted to ride horses of all calibers, so I ignored my anxiety and asked for a job. He took a chance on me as an exercise rider. It was hard work, seven days a week. Being up and on my first assigned horse and ready to gallop at 4:45 AM was not easy, but worth it.

Charlie was a contemporary man in many ways. In the early '80s, the track was a man's world and women exercise riders were unheard of. Amazingly enough, while I was there, Charlie had hired eight women riders! He called us Charlie's Angels. Thinking back, I was so fortunate to work at some great farms and training stables over the years.

I recall one incredible sunny day on the beautiful bridle paths at Point Reyes National Seashore. I was with a group of experienced horsewomen who knew the importance of not traveling off the trail. Certain paths were for horses and others for cyclists, none of which allowed both. The ladies and their horses were following my lead, taking pictures and enjoying the scenic views.

As we slowly gaited up the cliff, single file toward the hillside, out of nowhere four cyclists came ripping around the curve. As you would expect, the horses were startled. Lisa's horse spooked so badly it was about to go over the embankment. I pulled on the reins of her horse to prevent both of them from going over the steep cliff, all the while I was attempting to maintain the steadiness of my own horse. However, there was not enough room on that part of the trail for both horses at the same time. It was a slow-motion moment.

My trusted equine companion Noah and I began to free-fall down the steep shale cliff. It all happened so much faster than I could have imagined. We tumbled together, hitting heads and seeing the fear in each other's eyes. His leather reins slid through my fingers. I awkwardly grabbed a root and hung on, dangling for dear life. As Noah, the strong, young and muscular horse fell further down, he got hung up in the overgrown stinging nettle bushes. I could hear him calling out in desperation. It was awful. The sadness in his eyes and his cries of pain return to haunt me to this day.

All five of us who were on the trail tried helping him, to at least treat his discomfort and the allergic reaction he was having to the stinging nettles. Yet Noah continued to move violently due to his state of anaphylactic shock. He fought and flailed, getting himself hung up deeper into the dense brush. As he slid further down the sheer rock embankment, we could not save him; he fell 250 feet into the ocean below.

This was one of the worst days I ever experienced in my lifetime. To this day, my client Lisa still thanks me for saving her life, although in my mind, Noah will always be remembered as the ultimate hero that day. The cyclists never even circled back around to offer help. Afterwards, I took myself to the hospital with a concussion and a broken heart.

The very next day I rode in a dressage show with my dark brown, athletic-bodied Rhett. It was a pretty stupid decision because I wasn't paying attention to my body at all. My head was still swollen from the accident; I remember my helmet not fitting very well. This big-hearted horse and I had a deep spiritual connection together. It seems silly, but I needed him that day to help me get through the sadness I felt from losing Noah. It was worth it.

Over time, this body of mine began to understand shock. I can't tell you about the accidents I don't remember; there are quite a few of those because of my countless concussions. But there are many I do recall. Amerindio from Argentina bit off my index finger. I never blamed him; he had been mistreated before coming to stable with me. The van driver who brought him warned me he was a savage biter. Luckily, I was able to retrieve my finger from inside my glove and had it sewn back on. A few months later, Amerindio and I eventually found mutual trust when I helped him out of the muddy irrigation ditch he had fallen into.

I broke both legs with the same horse at different times in the same year. How funny is that? His name was Mr. Ecuador. My right leg broke when he spooked while we were trotting across an arena together. I only remember hearing the crack of my leg, nothing else. My left leg shattered months later when he decided to jump sideways while I was gently trying to take the stitches out of his right hind leg from a cut he experienced from the arena fencing. Being a trained vet technician, I knew holding up his left hind leg would prevent me from getting kicked, but Mr. Ecuador decided to thrust laterally, much to my surprise!

Both times I took myself to the hospital and hopped into the ER on my good leg, because I truly believe wheelchairs are for people who have had a major accident. Since *one* of my legs was working fine, I considered my damage minor. I still rode every day, even with a cast on. An old picnic table helped me get up and off whatever horse I was riding.

I guess my pain threshold is pretty high. If the discomfort becomes unbearable, I force my mind to find a calm place. A meadow with pretty purple lupines is what I like to visualize, my version of mind over matter meditation. People would say I was nuts or stubborn, but I just did what I needed to do for economic security, and to be with my equine buddies for emotional security.

A few years ago I was with Danny, my dark brown thoroughbred who is a practical joker, full of character. I was wearing street clothes, which was not smart. It made it much harder to stay on his back when he unexpectedly began to violently buck, resisting my instruction. He may have sensed my personal life was upsetting me, or he may have had a tummy ache caused by gas. Horses cannot "burp," so they rear and contort to get air out of their stomachs. Normally, I can stay on when that happens, but this time it was different.

I tried pulling Danny's head up, but my saddle slipped. Sliding down his shoulder, he slammed me into a round wooden post in the arena. Luckily, a groom found me lying unconscious. When I had landed, my neck hyper-flexed, pulling my spinal cord away from the ligaments, while fracturing three vertebrae. I was a bobble head, diagnosed with a broken neck and unable to ride for two years. It often amazes me that I am actually still alive.

Over the years, my body might break, but the connection I have to all my horses can never be fractured, cracked, or shattered. Horses are the loves of my life; they give me a purpose.

Although my heart has been broken many times, I feel full from all our crazy adventures and the joy I have experienced with these special steeds.

Today, I am gentler on myself than I used to be. It's not easy to slow down, but I'm trying. A smidgen of arthritis is the only thing that annoys me now. I continue to work at two farms, training mainly retired racehorses, giving them a second chance in either show-jumping, dressage, or as companion horses. I just sent Hansel, an aging thoroughbred with the kindest soul and big, calcified ankles, to use his talents with a children's handicapped riding group. Hansel offers these kids freedom of movement, and has found a home for life.

Over the years, I have learned so much from each horse. Even when I am tired and exhausted, these equines with different personalities and flowing manes and tails have a way of lighting up my world. They never judge or nit-pick me. I always prefer being in their company to human beings. My four-legged friends never make me feel unworthy. Our relationships are relaxed. Opening my heart to them has always been easy. My twenty-two-year-old daughter, Callie, shares a similar connection to and love of horses. It brings me joy to see how they have given her self-confidence and a form of relaxation as well.

Alamo Pintado is the newest love of my life. This dapple-gray with four tall white socks and big beautiful eyes experienced severe ulcers and had stopped eating. He had been through numerous owners and trainers when I bought him for $2,000. When we are out in the round pen together, I often think to myself, thank goodness we finally found each other! It is unreal how happy and healthy he is now. I always want what is best for the horses; their needs come first.

I take great pride in saying that most of my life has been spent on horseback, which, for me is the best seat with the best view—looking at the world between the ears of a horse.

Chapter Six

Clara

I feel blessed to know this extraordinary human, proficient in seven languages, a contemporary academic, renowned speaker, and an inspiration to all. Clara is ninety-years-young and a Holocaust survivor. For over a decade, I have been fortunate to observe firsthand how Clara is slowly healing the world with her message of hope.

Her mission is to educate others, advising everyone around her to be aware of what is happening in the world. As a wise mentor, she captures the attention of students of all ages with her stories of survival. Although young men and women may struggle to compre-hend the adversities she endured in her early life, they frequently realize these are not the stories found in their history books. Clara's accounts are priceless pieces of the past, and most of them are chronicled in her book, I Am Still Here: My Mother's Voice.

During the interview, my college-bound son came in and gave Clara a hug. She told him she would miss being able to call on him to troubleshoot her computer problems. Consistently paying him in "chocolate currency" was an arrangement the two of them worked out when he helped her purchase her Dell desktop many years earlier. She reminded him to stay focused and take his schooling seriously.

After our interview, Clara showed me a round ornamental plaque on her desk with the inscription, "Learn from the past. Live for the moment. Hope for the future." I am so grateful my sons have had the chance to know this amazing woman, a living reminder to me and my family that each of us can create a better world by learning to coexist with all cultures, races and religions. Inspired by her life, I regularly remind my children to recognize love, wisdom, beauty and truth in all people—whether they be friends, enemies, or strangers.

The guard lowered his hand and lifted my shirt. I felt sick. Tears were running down my face. Only my mother saw these tears. I could not run. They had guns. I was afraid. This was one of many times I would also feel demoralized and dispirited.

It was May 1944. The guards herded us from our village like animals. Thirty-nine members of my family came to the ghetto with us. Each family was divided by blankets; we slept side by side on the floor, crammed together like sardines. I remember overhearing my uncle explaining to my sobbing aunt why he wanted to die. Feeling the fear of the unknown, I too, began to cry out loud. Father took my hand to calm me down. My optimistic father always tried to keep our spirits up, despite the 10,000 of us now living in confinement.

Homeless now, any future we could imagine looked bleak. I felt thirsty all the time due to the heat. The lack of toilets was a problem. We used candles sparingly, not knowing how long we would be in the wretched brick factory where the German guards kept us penned. We had no freedom. We could not even speak to one another.

I gladly obeyed when, eventually, we were ordered out of the factory. I hated that place. As we walked to the train station, the other detainees warned us it would get worse. They explained that Auschwitz was not just a concentration camp but an extermination camp as well. I am not sure my family and I fully realized what they meant. Yet when we arrived at the camp and saw the misery, malnutrition, and death around us, we began to understand.

As soon as we stepped down from the packed cattle car, we heard the guards pointing at every person, "Go left… right…left…right, then right…right." Mama and me were going right and right again, together.

We learned after the war that to have been pointed in that direction kept us alive. I vividly remember pulling Mama to come with me. I was scared we would be separated when the next set of stern soldiers thoroughly examined her. Thankfully, she was healthy and looked younger than she really was. It was by sheer accident or good luck that my mother was chosen to stay with me and the other young girls. I was seventeen. She was forty-four.

Naked, we stood in line. We were told to keep our footwear on. I had hidden my boyfriend Ervin's picture in my right, black leather shoe, which gave me a small bit of comfort when I was being touched and inspected all over, and again when my curly chestnut hair was shaved off. As a young woman in our culture, I believed our hair is our crown. I still do now. I will never forget the Polish lady who sang while she shaved me like an animal. I felt completely disgraced. Mama did not even recognize me.

We were Jewish prisoners. Each of us was given one long straight grey dress, without panties or slip to wear. We were ordered to stand in lines of five deep, which was now our standard way of marching anywhere but mainly to work. Someone came with a brush and a big bucket of paint to put numbers on our backs. I was 51455. Mama and I barely escaped being tattooed with a number on our wrists, since tattoos were for those who stayed longer than a week at Auschwitz. We were there only eight dreadful days.

Dinner came in garbage cans filled with a pink colored liquid. This soup-like concoction tasted disgusting and was extremely salty. I remember thinking that someone would not feed this to pigs, yet I licked up every last drop. Drinking dirty rainwater from the leaky, rusty roofs helped to wash down the vile taste.

I remember seeing hundreds of bodies lying close together in the huge barracks. It was impossible to sleep. We were all in shock over what was happening around us. There were no latrines, only a ditch. We had no choice but to empty our bladders and bowels by squatting on soil and using long leaves as toilet paper. The German guards watched us closely with their hollow eyes. Pain and suffering surrounded us on all sides.

From Auschwitz, Mama and I were put on a ship going north to Riga, a small country in Northern Europe. During the trip, I remember seeing an unbelievable number of dead bodies thrown overboard into the cold grey Baltic Sea. Where all the bodies came from, I do not know.

When we arrived at Kaiserwald, another Nazi concentration camp, our job was to hand-cut batteries with a knife. We were told to take out the middle mushy stuff that would be used to make gunpowder. The aluminum and wires were recycled for other purposes. Working day and night, often women would fall asleep. Then they were shouted at or beaten with a bat to keep them awake. Mama and I kept our eyes wide open. I would sing Franz Lehar's love song, "Dein Ist Mein Ganzes Herz," ("Yours Is My Heart Alone") to help keep everyone awake.

Our ability to work kept us alive. Getting sick or appearing ill would cost us our lives. Our sole purpose was to provide labor for Hitler's war. If we could not do that, they disposed of us quickly.

Because of malnutrition and weight loss, most of the girls had stopped menstruating. I was one of the few who continued to have my period. I had to tear wide pieces of fabric from the bottom of my uniform to create a makeshift pad, using a longer ribbon of material as a belt to keep the pad in place.

Despite our wretched imprisonment, there were still moments of selfless humanity. I will never forget the kindness of a young German Jew who worked as a mechanic on the machines. Both of his parents had been killed before he arrived in Riga. He noticed my mother had lost a lot of weight and was looking extremely pale. This sympathetic young man gave me some red paper and told me to wet it and put it on Mama's cheeks. As an imitation rouge, it helped her look healthier than she really was. He also gave me a scarf to cover her bald head. Gestures like his made me believe there was still goodness out there in people.

Eventually, Mama and I were transferred once again. As we traveled to Stutthof, a concentration camp in Poland, I noticed my reflection in the window of the train. Our original uniforms had become laden with lice, yet I was even more disgusted by the new low-cut, green lace dress the guards gave me to wear. God only knows whose dress it was or where it came from. Mama said, "You look fine, Clara. Just imagine you are at a tea party, and you are the most beautiful girl there." I told her I looked like a prostitute.

Wearing my short cocktail dress and dirty, worn shoes, with a tattered blanket draped around me like a coat, I joined the other women digging anti-tank trenches intended to trap and tip over Russian tanks that never arrived. These trenches were six yards wide by six yards deep. In the frigid winter months the soil was frozen solid, which made it very difficult to use our shovels. Dynamite was introduced to help produce the gigantic ditches. These same explosives were utilized to create separate bigger holes—the ones where they made us bury the corpses.

January 19, 1945 came with the usual roll call and also a lesson about sacrifice. At that time, Mama seemed weaker than usual. Slowly, she pulled out a package wrapped in newspaper and in a low murmur said, "Happy 18th birthday, my darling." There in front of my listless eyes were three portions of bread put together with layers of margarine. My mother had not eaten her one-piece-a-day portion for three whole days in order to make me a layered birthday cake. It was the greatest present of my life. Let me remind you now: Never criticize or argue with your mother—she always has your best interest at heart.

Over 100 of us marched for two days with our German guards until we arrived at a farm in the middle of East Prussia. We overheard them explaining to the owner that the Russians were coming, and they needed to either burn us or shoot us. But the owner of the farm (we named him "Old Papa,") told them, "No! If you burn them the whole region will smell of human flesh, and if you shoot them, I will be left without bullets to protect myself." When we woke up the next day, we found ourselves without guards. They had left us alone. We were free. Old Papa was a very good man.

When the war ended with the help of the Allies, Hitler's Germany was finally defeated. Now it was time to go home. Ahead of us was an excruciating three-month walk from what is now modern-day Poland to our village in Transylvania, Romania. Without maps or compasses, we had to ask for directions every day.

Desperation left us no choice but to cautiously trust the people we encountered. On the road we once met a Jewish soldier who warned us not to stay too long in one of the small cities we were heading toward. He also reminded Mama and me to be careful who we accepted favors from, since rape was a major concern. If we were lucky, during our journey from Poland to Romania, we would find a stable with animals or an empty attic where we could get a good night's sleep. Food was scare, but the thrill of freedom kept us moving forward one step at a time!

Arriving home I was still wearing the sturdy leather shoes my father, a shoemaker, had made for me. Inside our house we found only our mattresses and my brother Zoltan's piano; these were the only items not taken from us. Mama and I both knew in our hearts we would all be together here soon. Father told us back in the ghetto that if we were ever separated not to worry, since we would find our way back home. I still see his face at the train station in Auschwitz looking at me, waving and smiling as if to simply say, "See you later."

We learned that father survived the horrid camp conditions and the death of Zoltan, only to die of typhoid fever on his walk home in May 1945. Knowing that he was so close to keeping his promise was difficult to deal with. A boy with a Hebrew name who lived in our village shared my father's and my brother's stories with us. As a pianist, Zoltan refused to break the stones that were used to create roads between camps to protect his hands. Consequently, he was shot in front of my father after the first few days, trying to speak to a soldier in his broken German. We never did see or hear from the other members of our family after we were separated at the ghetto.

It was just Mama and me now.

I remember a powerful conversation I had with my father on my sixteenth birthday, two years before any of this happened. In the middle of my party, we went outside into the garden. It was bitterly cold sitting on the cement bench under our apple tree. He spoke to me about the rumors of war, which he had heard about on his radio hidden in our basement. He told me, "Listen, you are sixteen years old. Promise me you will not get married until you have your diploma in hand. They can take everything away from you, but they cannot take away your education."

I finished my studies with my beloved father in mind. I graduated from college in 1950 with a degree in French, English and the History of Art in the Middle Ages. Education has been my life. After fifty years, I eventually retired from teaching, although I still teach French two days a week at the retirement community where I live.

Mama stayed with me her entire life. We had an exceptionally rare relationship. She was my support through a deep depression after my dear husband Paul died unexpectedly in a workplace accident. As a pharmaceutical chemist, he was working at a plant he owned in Queens, New York. A piece of machinery accidently fell on him. Paul was an exceptional man, and we were married forty years. He understood the unbreakable bond Mama and I shared. She and I were never apart until her death at 101 years of age.

On my ninetieth birthday, California Lutheran University recognized me for my contributions to education and peace. I was honored and elated to have the University acknowledge my life's work, and announce the Clara Knopfler Jewish Leadership Scholarship to benefit the education of future generations of Jewish students. Both Rachel and Robert, my grandchildren to whom I dedicated my book, were present, as well as my son George. Surrounded by three generations of family, how I wish Mama had been there beside me, too. After all, the honor was partly hers. She helped me get through life; I stood tall for her there.

I share my story in order to educate and inspire as many people as I possibly can. Please promise me you will tell my story to your children. And tell your children they must tell it to their children as well. My mission has always been to make sure people do not forget the worst genocide in the history of mankind. It must never happen again. As my father told me years ago, no one can ever take your education away from you. I truly believe that education and understanding lead to acceptance and coexistence.

Chapter Seven

Annette

A long-limbed brunette in a sleeveless tangerine shift dress sashayed down the runway wearing a wide-brimmed ivory and orange Derby hat, adorned with assorted feathery flowers. It was Temecula Fashion Week. This master milliner and owner of "Annette's Couture" was presenting eighteen vibrantly sophisticated hats. Who would ever guess that this was her first runway show?

The professional models strutted to the sounds of Maroon 5, Bruno Mars, and Justin Timberlake, each sporting a one-of-a-kind creation. With an innate talent for pairing women with hats, each handmade design had its own aesthetic appeal, unified by Annette's whimsical, refined, and completely chic charm. Her show created quite a buzz among the local news media, photographers, and social media bloggers. I wanted to be wearing one of her haute hats myself!

A few weeks later we connected, and she kindly indulged my countless questions. An Eastern European beauty from the country of Georgia (next to Russia, not the state next to Florida), Annette has a ravenous desire for knowledge. However, her master's degree in foreign languages and linguistics didn't exactly prepare her to be a milliner—clearly a career twist she is passionate about. I was gobsmacked by her fabulous designs and her flair for the ever-evolving fashion world.

Somehow, I felt completely at ease in the presence of her non-stop motion. She pulled "her version" of a traditional Georgian cheese-filled bread called khachapuri *out of the oven, and brewed the tastiest of teas using dried hibiscus flowers her mother sends monthly from Russia. Annette talked about living during Soviet-occupied times. She describes how difficult it is for anyone to understand the level of corruption, uncertainty, and economic stress if they didn't experience it for themselves.*

Drinking my tea, I noticed her brass soldering iron sitting alongside various pieces of red crinoline on her dining room table workspace. Together with hand painted white and red feathers, this was a new design in progress that would crown the head of one lucky client at the Breeder's Cup the following month.

Annette is a self-proclaimed perfectionist and her own worst critic. "Being a very detailed person can be a challenge," she confides to me. "Each hat I make must be impeccable."

I was beginning to understand how her methodology of design and form originate from a confluence of her education, personal drive, and her family's history with fashion. I gathered from her stories that there has always been a creative energy tucked inside just trying to emerge. In millinery, she seems to have finally found the perfect outlet!

My hat career started when a woman on Coronado Island asked where I had gotten the turquoise bucket hat I was wearing. A friend who was with me quickly chimed in, "She made it herself!" The startled woman queried if I made them for sale, and later that day I found myself thinking: Well, why not try?

In my thirties, I found all I wanted to do was create things. I dabbled with crocheting, knitting, sewing, cross-stitching, embroidering, baking cookies with royal icing—my hands are like me, never still! I have always loved hats, but finding them in my size was continually a challenge. So I decided to start designing and building my own.

Hats felt like a natural outlet for my creativity, and they felt natural as a potential business outlet as well. My mother is a fashionista herself, in addition to being a talented dress designer. As a seamstress, she never used a pattern or took measurements. She could look at me and make me a dress in one night. My father was a shoe designer who ran a private shoe manufacturing business in Russia. Maybe that is why I chose hats—I wanted to explore something different! And I've found the possibilities with hats are endless.

In the beginning, my husband grumbled that "my hobby" was getting expensive, as the costs of millinery material, blocks, and feathers added up. My first year, I sold eight of the ten hats I took to a boutique located in a nearby beach community. The owner marked the price up three times and did not reimburse me appropriately. I knew then that I needed to sell directly to customers.

The next year, I opened an online store through Etsy and sold fifteen hats. Last year I sold almost eighty, for prices that had tripled over the last five years. I had to close my online store three weeks before the Derby, turning down customers, since one person alone can't possibly handle that many orders. My husband doesn't grumble anymore, although he does remind me that I yell a bit more during high hat season. But it is no longer just my hobby; it's a growing, profitable business!

I'm a very hard worker—a trait that was ingrained in me during my childhood. In Georgia, education was free, yet highly competitive. Academic expectations of me were very high, especially from my mother. I was lectured every time I got a B instead of an A. As a result, I put immense pressure on myself and, despite my ulcers I usually succeeded.

While in school, girls were taught to sew, and boys would learn woodworking. I recall taking caramel-colored kitchen towels and sewing them into an apron. In addition to daily schoolwork, I also received seven years of music training, three times a week, for two or three hours a day, specializing in classical piano. I remember performing Mozart's Sonata No. 5 in front of hundreds of people. I learned at an early age how to keep my poise under pressure.

I remember I received one B that almost impeded my admission into the Foreign Institute at Tbilisi State University, where I studied for five years. I specialized in foreign languages, which was one of the top three areas of study, along with law and medicine.

At the University, I met a fine-looking man with a distinct Bavarian accent. When he asked me to marry him, I agreed, although three days prior to the wedding, I realized he was not the right match for me. But with 250 guests invited, and my father being a very recognized and respected man among his family and friends, I decided to take a chance and go ahead with the wedding. It took me a very long minute or two to sign the marriage certificate. I can still remember my newlywed husband's face, looking at me with critical concern.

After finishing my studies, I was offered an opportunity to work at the Marco Polo Hotel, the first five-star, foreign-built facility in my home country of Georgia. Growing up in the USSR, I acquired most of my information from books, not personal experiences. Meeting real people from countries I had only read about changed the way I looked at the world. I had real life experiences with so many different cultures and interacted with so many important people: the president of Georgia, diplomats and ambassadors, at least fifty US Senators, presidents and CEOs of huge corporations, as well as the elite of Tbilisi, the capital city where the hotel was located. The KGB, which was the main security agency for the Soviet Union, would often close the hotel to the public due to high security alerts when certain gatherings were taking place with VIP's.

That first job made me who I am now: a confident woman who loves and respects herself. I learned to be adamant about achieving my goals, along with believing in my dreams. I know for a fact, if you put your mind to it, everything will happen for you!

When Russia cut my country off from gas and water, my family was forced to move. My oldest son Robert, the best gift from my first marriage, was born in 1992. When he was one-year-old, I had to send him to Russia to live with my family. The economic situation was worsening in Georgia and a civil war was in progress. Russian tanks were in the streets and the city was full of mafia. However, the hotel was busier than ever, full of reporters from around the world.

I was earning a substantial salary at the hotel, so I chose to stay. I would work a month straight, then take a month off to be with Robert. I also helped my parents purchase a house in Russia, while I continued to work in Georgia. Yet physically and emotionally, it was an extremely hard time for me. The separation from my little boy was the absolute worst.

When my well-paying job ended abruptly, I moved in with my family. After a long overdue divorce, it was time for me to devise a new plan to support my son and me. Now that I valued myself as a strong, capable woman, and longed for new and different prospects, I knew I wanted to move to the United States. Further, the difficulty of living with my parents and depending on them after so many years of being self-sufficient expedited my decision.

I immigrated because of economic reasons, yes, but I loved the American culture as well. Having visited America years before, I fell in love with San Diego, so I applied for a tourist visa. I left Robert, who was almost seven by this time, in Russia while I looked for work in California. The first three years were the most difficult, missing my son while working multiple jobs taking care of other peoples' children as a nanny. But I made enough money to support myself and send some back home to my family as well.

My second husband, Patrick was everything I was looking for in a man. At first, our nine-year age gap and different cultural backgrounds tested the strength of the relationship. Yet he was mature, responsible, and family oriented. Unlike my first husband who was still a child in many ways, unwilling to take on the responsibilities of providing for and loving his family, Patrick showed me how loving and generous a man could be. When Robert was thirteen, we brought him to live with us. After dealing with almost two years of endless paperwork and an international lawyer, Patrick officially adopted him as his son.

In life, I never look back. Today I am very happy with the juggling act of being a wife and mother of two boys, in addition to slowly expanding my home-based millinery business. I am most productive and focused at night when everyone is sleeping. Years of intense studying and training in school primed me for long, laborious hours of hat making—and our house is wonderfully quiet at three o'clock in the morning!

I've also become very adept at dodging my six-year-old, Edgar as he races around the house wearing his spiky Mohawk helmet, shooting Nerf guns at me, while I attempt to glue a delicate goose feather on my latest creation. Stress actually brings out my muse. I remember when Patrick changed jobs a few years ago creating five new designs was a great release and therapy for me.

Once I decide to do something, I give it my all, and hats are no exception. "Traditional formal" is how I would describe my designs. A hint of avant-garde, in certain sections, but I prefer structure. Each fashionable shape I configure is unique. I do not want any of my hats to be the same, nor do I stick to one style; that approach would be too boring for me. I am always devising ways to control costs, while maintaining a quality product.

It is vital that my clients are happy; together we design a hat that suits them. I prefer to think through the entire artistic process before I begin working, as I determine what type of hat will suit each individual woman. My styles range from simple fascinators—light ornamental headpieces consisting of feathers, flowers or beads typically attached to a comb, hair clip or even a headband—to Grand Derby hats.

When choosing a hat, the shape of a woman's face and her overall height need to be taken into consideration. Tall women can wear almost any shape or kind of hat: a down or upturn, a small or wide brim. Petite women have certain guidelines, such as no downturned or wide-brimmed hats. What complements their smaller structure is an upturned brim, especially a saucer design, or any type of fascinator that makes one appear taller. Cocktail or percher hats are nice for smaller women, too.

Thanks to Kate Middleton (aka Catherine, Duchess of Cambridge), right now fascinators are in vogue. The dress one will wear with the hat often dictates my inspiration for a new design. I am of the school of thought that believes the dress and the hat must *complete* each other, not *compete*. There has to be a balance.

It has been fun to watch my hats encircle the globe. Women have worn my creations in Great Britain, Germany, France, Italy, the Czech Republic, in addition to other European countries, as well as in Australia, and throughout North and South America. The Kentucky Derby in May is one of my busiest times. I have also had ladies wear my hats to the Royal Ascot in England, which is an incredible honor for me. The racetracks at Churchill Downs and Del Mar are also popular venues, as are countless weddings and various other special occasions where one might wish to don a classy *chapeau*.

My goal is not to be famous, just an admired and skilled hat maker. I have received invitations to collaborate with other designers, or be a part of various runways and shows in Los Angeles, New York and Las Vegas—but we'll see. My son, Edgar, is still young, and my family is my priority. Yet, hats will always be fashionable. For now, I am happy being a one-woman show, creating not just another fashion accessory, but a unique, wearable work of art.

Leilah

As I sit at my desk preparing to write this story, I notice the cobalt blue glass bottle filled with a homemade essential oil elixir on the bookshelf. I spray a bit in the room and breathe in the refreshing mist, feeling it immediately clear my muddled mind. The crafty looking label states: Motivating Mist—Made with Love by Leilah.

Like her special concoction of lemon and peppermint, Leilah is a therapeutic presence for me. In addition to her infectious laugh and precise yoga poses, I admire how sincerely and intensely she listens to the people around her, really hearing what they are saying. One of our very first conversations was over a glass of pink Prosecco. My pending surgery was making me a bit nervous, and I told her I thought hospitals should really offer a glass of bubbly to all patients and guests upon entering. She shared with me her belief in angels guiding and protecting us.

A few weeks later she brought me a beautifully wrapped box. Tucked inside was the Encyclopedia of Angels, *along with a petite bag of champagne-laced gummy bears. The handwritten card in flowy cursive script read, "A book and bubbles to help heal and assist you through your surgical procedure. I hope you enjoy this guide containing over 200 celestial beings." Her thoughtfulness brought tears to my eyes. She has a natural way of caring for others, making them feel special.*

Months later, Leilah trusted me enough to tell me about her past. With a cool, calm, and collected demeanor, she disclosed ages and stages in her life that were not easy to talk about. Many quiet moments elapsed during that sunset walk on the beach, while we both absorbed the magnitude of her revelations. One in particular left us both standing as still as statues staring out to sea as the sun silently dipped below the horizon. We turned simultaneously to resume our quiet walk, yet in my typically preoccupied fashion, I immediately stumbled over a pile of rocks.

Looking down, we both saw that I had actually tripped on an oversized circle of stones, encompassing a strikingly appropriate peace sign in the center. For Leilah, this was a timely reminder of when she discovered her missing piece within her interpersonal relationships. Rising up from the mayhem and madness of her past, she has taught herself to be the sunshine when the light cannot be found.

Even though Leilah was not ready to talk about certain details, she did recognize that in many ways the physical, sexual, emotional, and spiritual abuse she survived has made her the gutsy girl she is today. This story is only a fraction of what she has actually endured.

As we continued our walk toward town, she commented on how abandoning old notions of unworthiness can be so challenging. When the streetlights gradually flickered on, we both agreed a café on the opposite corner looked welcoming. While each of us waited for our piece of German chocolate cake to arrive, Leilah went on to explain how working through abuse and acknowledging fear were the best ways to release the tight grip they held on her.

Our cake arrived and after only one bite, we decided the coconut-pecan icing was one of the finest we had ever had. Leilah's story helps me to remember that no matter what we're going through, we always need to make room for forgiveness, love, and the sweet things in life.

Once upon a time there was a beautiful young princess who was kept as a prisoner by five wacky witches.

This might sound silly, I know. But in many ways my childhood was like the sad pages of many fairy tales, the part just before "happily ever after." In my early childhood, I experienced so much suffering that I have never wanted to have a lengthy conversation describing everything that happened to me, except perhaps with my four brothers and three sisters, who shared these painful times. I do know that the physical and emotional abuse I suffered at the hands of multiple family members, combined with the neglect of other family members, significantly influenced me in ways that I still struggle with as an adult.

I don't know if my circumstances were worsened because of social or cultural clashes. When I was very young we moved to the Unites States from Baghdad, Iraq. My father, Baba had his eyes focused on the financial well-being of not only his wife and eight children, but his extended family as well. To soothe the stress this caused him, Johnny Walker walked home from work with him every night. Something that seemed so strange to me, even now reflecting back, is how Baba would look right *through* me. He never really saw me.

Even stranger, my father never laid one finger on us. He was also unaware his sisters were physically beating us. Mama was present too, and received the same abuse from the witches. She was frequently subservient, allowing herself to be victimized not only by her husband, but her shifty sisters-in-law.

Almost every single day, a certain type of thrashing occurred to at least one of us. Some whippings drew blood and left open wounds; others just welts. Yet always what was left was a bruising and discoloration of our skin.

A perceptive neighbor boy dubbed Baba's five cruel siblings "the wacky witches." Like in Shakespeare's play *Macbeth*, the female witches constantly tempt the king, setting into motion the events that culminate in tragedy. However, in our tiny wicked kingdom, the calamity was exclusively unleashed upon the "king's" offspring. There was so much indefinable aggression and loathing especially aimed at me and my siblings. It made me wish every day that the witches would just dissolve into thin air and disappear.

Lying alone in my sterile white-walled bedroom, my body bruised and my heart broken, I remember longing for a prince, or a good fairy, or anyone to come and rescue my siblings and me. But more than that, I longed to live a normal life like my friends at school. The strict rules imposed by the witches, not Baba, meant I couldn't play outside, go to social events, or take part in any sports or after-school programs. There were so many double standards in our home, yet the girl-versus-boy roles were the ones that aggravated me the most.

My brothers played football and I always wanted to join them. Gymnastics very much interested me as well. In physical education class, I would get a little taste of what it felt like to be an athlete and participate as part of a team. And I loved it! Thank goodness I wasn't restricted from *watching* the Olympics. I dreamt of being Mary Lou Retton, soaring through the air feeling free and light, perfectly balanced in body and mind.

It was agonizing watching my brothers play sports and ride skateboards outside with their friends, while I sat inside doing nothing for hours. One day I decided to join them. The wacky witches were away. I knew I would get in trouble, but I was determined that the experience would be worth whatever the consequences might be. It was a breathtaking forty-five minutes of freedom when I sat on a skateboard, while my brother's friend pushed me down the street over and over again. It felt awesome.

When the witches came home and saw that I had escaped, I was dragged back into the house by my long braided hair.

I had disobeyed their rule: girls do not go outside to play. Once inside, they spun me by my braid like a whirly top. I actually levitated off the ground. How my hair did not all come out is still a mystery to me. Based on the regular beatings that occurred, this isolated experience left me feeling nothing but numb once more.

Verbal assaults were also a daily occurrence. I was called stupid and told I would never amount to anything. Sometimes I was labeled fat. Other times the witches told me I was so ugly I looked like a boy. Which made me think, if I looked so much like a boy, why couldn't I go play outside like one? Countless times I was tempted to say this, but I never did.

The only rules Baba imparted on his children, especially us girls, were the basic Middle Eastern ones: no promiscuous clothing; no going out with boys; no talking back to any adults, ever; and waiting to have an arranged marriage. The witches had cast a spell over my father long ago. The lies they told him were atrocious. The most ridiculous of their tall tales was about me being a "boy magnet." How *could* I be? I lived like a prisoner. The witches accused me of something different every day.

Never did I do anything worthy of the punishments I received. Mama knew I was innocent. Sometimes I think Baba did too. I never understood, and still don't, why my parents did not intervene to protect their children. My father's sisters were vile, nasty human beings. Staying strong was not easy, but I was determined to show my aunts that they could not turn me into a likeness of them. I promised myself that I would never become angry, bitter, and full of revenge.

Of course, I wanted the violence to stop. My siblings and I had very few days without some type of beating. The witches' punishments came in all forms; sometimes it was their bare hands slapping or scratching our skin. A beating could also be with whatever they could get a hold of at the moment: a belt, fly swatter, or my rubber shoes. To this day when I order shish kabobs in a restaurant, seeing them brings back the sensation of being burned by that metal stick.

I wanted to fight back. My muscles constantly twitched, quelling my own rage. Adrenaline rushed through my veins; every cell in my brain screamed, *fight back!* But I knew I was outnumbered; it was five witches against me, hitting me until I cried and moaned uncontrollably. Eventually, I began to notice the pattern. The quicker I began to cry, their repeated strikes became fewer, and the sooner the abuse would stop. This strategy became my best defense during those ten-to thirty-minute beatings.

Can you imagine being whipped on your back with a glass Coke bottle? That was a frequent occurrence. While it was happening, I would travel outside of myself to a different place. I would imagine an ornate palace with beautiful gardens and crystal chandeliers, without the eerie echoes of the witches. When the final smack ricocheting through my body brought me back to reality, I was always relieved that the bottle hadn't broken.

What did break was my heart. Not from endless batterings, although my body was in a constant state of recovering from whippings. My heart was broken because I longed to escape, and I couldn't. I fantasized about what life would be like outside my four walls, far from the witches' reach. I dreamed of how it would feel to truly experience life, like having a slumber party with a friend, or playing on a sports team. My classmates constantly asked me why I couldn't go to social events with them. It was very embarrassing, since there were never enough excuses. I was being held hostage in my own house by my own family.

In order to survive, my siblings and I took refuge in each other. Our shared room became a safe sanctuary, although it was a small space that only allowed for two double bunk beds on opposite walls. Humor was our only coping mechanism. Poking fun at the witches was our secret pastime. We gave them nicknames: Bad Breath, Lizard Lips, White Leg, Penny Pincher, Flesh Worm. Bad Breath was the ringleader who provoked all the aggression against us.

We would try to get revenge by setting booby traps in the carpet with the serrated edge from the aluminum foil carton. We would carefully tear it from the packaging, cut it into tiny pieces and nestle one or two into the shag carpeting. The witches would step on these three-inch sharp setups with their bare feet and flinch. Yet never once did they suspect us. I sometimes wonder why we did not try to overtake them when the daily beatings started. Together, there were more of us than them.

I feel very vulnerable sharing detailed descriptions of what went on so many years ago in my family. The cruel environment I grew up in affected my personality, to be sure.

It took me a long time to understand that people can be kind, families can be loving and supportive, and parents want their children to flourish. My norm was definitely different. I am still trying to mentally distance myself from the pain of my childhood suffering.

One thing I knew for sure was that making money would be my ticket out of hell. It would get me away from my family and still allow me to support them financially, which is customary in our culture. The abuse, at least physically, stopped when I was a senior in high school. I started working as an after-school counselor with children ages five to twelve, when I was eighteen. At that time, I also convinced Baba to let me get my college degree. Finally, I began to live and experience a real life.

It was difficult adjusting outside the confines of my residential "penitentiary." There was so much I didn't understand, because I didn't have any experience growing up in the "real" world. I was learning everything for the first time as a freshman in college. I had never been in a relationship, and some of the men I dated preyed on my innocence and naivety. They took advantage of me sexually, emotionally, and financially. A series of unfortunate events took place that I am still not ready to talk about. All I will say is that I trusted the wrong people. I realized that my long social isolation had deeply affected my judgment.

I decided to begin seeing a therapist who wanted me to delve deeper into my dysfunctional upbringing, yet I knew that the damage had been done. I wanted to move forward, despite the tensions still being present in my family members.

At this time in my life, the situation is different. Although I am still living in the same house, I like to say my parents live with *me* now. A few of my siblings still live in the house as well, so they can help our parents when I am out working or traveling. When I am home, I love it when my sisters and I get together and reminisce, talking about all we have been through, but never feeling sorry for ourselves.

Only four witches are left. Their power has been stripped, and they are barely involved in our lives. Ties have been broken; communication with them has ceased. I avoid family gatherings if they are ever present. Within our nuclear family, there is limited drama now. We are focusing on the next generation, making sure my twenty-three-year-old niece and my eight-year-old nephew never have to experience what we went through.

Part of me wants to move out of the house now, but I have made the decision to support my elderly parents. It is how I was raised. As Mama and Baba grow older and their health conditions worsen, it makes it harder for me to leave. If I did go out on my own, I know I would feel so much guilt in my newfound freedom knowing Baba would continue to cause Mama pain. When I am around, his behavior is kinder to her. My siblings help as much as they can in different ways when they can afford it. But I am single; they are not. They have spouses and families to support; I do not.

Over the last ten years, I have started to slowly restore my self-image. Practicing yoga is my safe space, a sanctuary where I can heal my body, mind, and spirit. I don't want to be a victim of circumstances. I feel that I am beginning to transcend the trauma I experienced. Looking at myself in the oversized mirror doing a tree pose, I feel focused as I strive for balance. I concentrate on how far I have come, instead of how far I have left to go.

Growing up the way I did, I never imagined I would be able to drive or purchase my own car, let alone obtain certification to be a Reiki Master practitioner. The main purpose of attaining that hands-on wellness training was to heal myself, but now I can also assist others in their healing.

A few years ago, I participated in the Ironman Triathlon. It took a great deal of mental strength to continue, even when my body told me to stop. I am certain if you truly believe you can do something, nothing will stop you. I worked hard to get my degree, and each job I have had has paid me well. I have proven to myself that I am stronger than the wacky witches. Stronger even than Baba.

As a young girl, all I wanted to hear from Baba and Mama was, "I love you." Those three powerful words that many people freely say, and sometimes take for granted, I have longed for all my life. I have yet to hear them say this to me. I am forty-four now. Love to me has seemed chaotic, confusing, and painful. Still I stay hopeful and continue to search for that genuine love, caring and affection that will fill me with the longed-for warmth, pleasure, safety, and peace.

One of my childhood dreams recently came true because I made it happen. I have been a diehard Charger football fan ever since I was a kid. And I always wanted to attend a game on Thanksgiving. This year I was able to watch my favorite team play on Thanksgiving Day in Dallas. This was my own version of fantasy football. The Chargers even won! I sat next to the nicest woman who was a Dallas Cowboys fan and she whispered to me after the game, "I secretly wanted them to win for you!"

Slowly but surely, I am crafting my "happily ever after" ending.

Trish

The nail salon is busy every time I walk in. Trish greets me with an unassuming smile and we begin our one-hour, face-to-face, heart-to-heart time together. Surrounding us are the standard salon accoutrements: vibrating massage recliners, stacks of celebrity magazines, shelves of O.P.I. nail polish arranged in a rainbow pattern, and of course, ceaseless chattering among women.

Often language barriers can keep us strangers as we suspiciously ponder what the other is saying. Trish and I may not share the same native language, but we share a lot of the same issues. Over the course of many monthly conversations, we have consoled one another, while comparing notes out of our personal playbooks. Yes, we gossip a bit, too. But mostly we just express to each other how we wish our children, husbands, and in-laws came with their own instruction manuals!

Born in Vietnam, raised in Germany, and for the past eleven years living in the United States, English is Trish's fourth language after Vietnamese, German and Cantonese. She is a fast learner, and has brought her adaptability and flair to a number of careers over the years. Trish has been crossing borders, both literal and cultural, her whole life, yet she confesses that raising her two young boys makes those challenges seem easy!

Every parent knows that there are plenty of opinions about how to raise children effectively, which can leave any mother or father completely overwhelmed. She admits that she is continuously looking for alternative ways of caring for Jaden and Hayden, ages eight and four, while desperately trying to include her husband in her efforts to support and nurture their little superheroes. During our conversations, Trish and I have also deliberated together on how annoying mothers-in-law can be when they interfere, since typically they always want things their way. I am grateful that the opportunity to open up and share our similar experiences has been a valuable means of vulnerability and camaraderie between the two of us.

Trish guides anyone who is willing to pay attention and heed her humble advice. She has mentioned to me the difficulties of finding the right Vietnamese words to communicate with her co-workers at times. I noticed that was true watching this meek, but not weak woman in action. It's not always a language barrier but a lack of understanding between her co-workers and clients that can obstruct dialogue and result in confusion. Once decoded however, there appears to be a collective effort to communicate through fragmented murmuring together.

To me, Trish is the ultimate communicator. Even if she is not the most fluent in English or Vietnamese, what she says and why she says it, really does matter. Words aren't the only vehicle to understanding each other. Trish taught me to be patient, listen, and take time to comprehend—all three are part of communicating, living and working with people. She is a remarkably useful ambassador of these traits.

Every day, I am learning! I learn from everyone—my husband, elders, co-workers, clients, even my children. Sometimes this is easy, but usually it is very hard and takes much patience.

In Germany, I was known as *Erzieherin,* educator. Education has always been important to me, and especially so when I went to college for teaching. In my classroom, there was a sweet two-year-old boy, one of the youngest. I liked him a lot. He had a little lisp when he spoke; where he placed his tongue when speaking was different than the other children. The Germans call it *lispeln.*

In Germany, they have an alternative higher education system where you can work and teach at the same time. It is like on-the-job training here in the US. I would go to school and after my classes, I taught twenty-six children, ages two to five. My mom was the one who suggested I pursue this approach to get my degree in teaching.

My early life was hard. My father abused my mother. In turn, she did not give me much love, and left Vietnam for Germany after I was born. I lived with my grandmother until the Communists took over. She was my mother figure and showed me warmth and affection. My father eventually went to prison, but no one ever told me why. I have little memory of this part of my childhood, yet I know it was not happy. I remember just one thing that made me happy: air conditioning. I was glad we had it in my grandmother's house; not everyone did.

When I was about five, my grandparents, my grand-mother's sister and I moved to Herten, Germany. We lived there with my mother and her new husband. I remember at seven, my heart fluttered when I fell in love for the first time. I will never forget that boy saying to me, "You are the prettiest in the classroom."

At twelve, I took care of my step-siblings. I was the boss, always deciding what we should do that day, or who should do what, when. What I would have liked more was to be outside all day, doing what I wanted to do, or be alone with my mystery books. Rarely did that ever happen.

Around the age of thirteen, I began to visit my relatives in the United States. I remember one time flying with my brother when the dinner service started. I felt sick and quickly tried to get to the restroom, but I did not make it. My brother was so embarrassed. I was, too.

I also remember not liking the food in the US very much. Where I came from in Germany, we had the best food! And I was a picky eater. My aunts did not know how to cook, so we usually ate out. I really liked sushi the first time I tried it. Italian food was my favorite. Now I often make lasagna for our family dinners.

My relatives wanted me to stay in America, especially my loving grandma. She had been living in the US for a number of years and separation from her was very hard for me. When I was twenty, I returned here again to be with her, yet I could stay for only ninety days with a work visa. I was employed at a Vietnamese coffee shop, *Café Giot Dang* in San Diego, California. This is where I first saw my future husband.

Minh ordered an ice café. He had nice dark brown eyes and black hair. There was no talking between us. We only made eye contact, and I remember waving goodbye when he walked out of the coffee shop that day. Then I decided to go back to Germany to finish school. But he told me later that he went back to the coffee shop many times to find me.

When I returned to the US a few years later, I filled out paperwork to become a citizen. It took six months, but I went back to work at *Café Giot Dang*. And there was Minh. Our eyes met again and there were nerves in my stomach. He asked for my number and we dated. He too was born in Vietnam and had moved to the United States when he was sixteen. Since I do not like men that talk too much, Minh seemed good for me. We married that same year.

Many Vietnamese women, especially the older generation, believe that the husband is number one. They listen to their man and they never talk back. Not me! My husband is a good man. He is honest, straightforward, and has a secure job working with computers. But he mostly says things without thinking, especially when he talks to his own mother and our children. This bothers me and makes me mad. I tell him that.

His mother did not help him with this habit growing up, and she does not lead by example. Instead, she knows my husband lacks this skill and takes advantage of it. She tells me, "All his words come from me." I try to explain to my husband how I see his mother, and the importance of learning to hear both sides. I think Minh needs to make up his own mind on who is correct. The problem is his parents always think they are right. Even if I try to explain my thoughts and go against them, I am on the hate list. If I am wrong or right, it is okay. It is my own opinion, and I will still say it. Of course I am polite to everyone, no matter what.

It is important to me that my husband open up his opinions to hear me and the kids when we talk to him. He never learned this growing up. I keep trying to teach him and talk to him about better ways to parent, especially not to yell or manipulate our sons. He will learn, not quickly, but slow— better than never, I guess.

My mother-in-law does not like the way I parent our boys, Jaden and Hayden. It does not bother me. I straight talk to my mother-in-law, but always with manners. If she is rude, I tell her we need to deal with things and solve them smoothly. From talking with friends and clients at work, I am learning that I am not alone in this problem. Their mothers-in-law are not always nice either.

I tell my boys to always talk and act with manners. I try at work and home to be an example of politeness and show them how to talk nicely. I am always straight and fair. I believe that is how respect is gained. I do not understand why people choose to say things not directly to the other person, only behind them. I do not like this behavior. All the time, I politely ask my husband, my in-laws, and even the women at work to talk to me directly, and please be clear.

I once tried to talk to Jaden's second grade teacher during a parent conference. I explained to her that he had a hard time paying attention, and was always trying to get out of the dining room chair when he was doing homework. I asked if this was normal. I asked for her help and if she had any ideas for me. She said nothing. I then went to the principal and tried again to explain my struggles with Jaden not sitting still and doing his homework. It felt like they didn't understand me; this was frustrating.

I remember helping a little boy in my classroom in Germany with math. He would never sit still and would not write his letters, just like Jaden. I understand it is hard for them at that young age; they just want to talk and play.

A few weeks later, the teacher tells me, "Well, at recess Jaden pushed another boy." Again, I was frustrated. Why had they ignored my concerns before? It was sad to me how the teacher and principal were not helpful to me and my son. I should have told them that I was a kindergarten teacher for four years and I understand their job! I made Jaden understand how being unkind is not the answer. There had to be consequences to his actions, so he did not get to play until he behaved better and stopped pushing other children.

It was at this time that our doctor diagnosed Jaden with ADHD. I had no idea what ADHD was, so I started reading books and talking with other people. I found out that my aunt's friend, Que, had a son with ADHD, too! Thinking back, the little boy who struggled in Germany showed similar signs like my son.

Every child is different. I do believe there is no normal. So I began talking to Jaden in a calmer voice, trying to explain to him different ways of doing things and why. I did not do that in the beginning.

Before he was taking medication, Jaden would never sit still. He was always moving his body. Any timeout for him was hell. He would hit himself, the sofa, or the wall. I am still not sure about the medication, but it has been easier with him since he started taking it. He is listening better and thinking before he acts. We are working on that together.

The other day, Jaden noticed a homeless man and asked me, "Why he is out there?" I explained, "People mess up in life or some do not have opportunities like you do, Jaden. Maybe when that man was a little boy, he did not have a mother to encourage him to do his homework. So you must listen and work hard." I tell him it is important to have a strong education because it is difficult to find a good-paying job. I say, "Because you are young now, you have to pay attention and study!"

We have many rules in our house. We limit cartoon watching and encourage more time playing outside. I know Jaden and Hayden watch actors and their behaviors on the computer or on television shows and copy what they see. This is not good for them.

It is important for our boys to stay on a schedule. When I am working only a few days a week, my husband will undo all of the hard work I put into changing our boys' behavior. This causes me so much stress. I try to teach him what I am doing, but I sometimes feel very alone when I am parenting.

One time when I was at work, Jaden called and told me what had just happened at home. It was hard for me to hear this story from him. Minh had called Jaden an asshole. I cried a lot, and I was very, very sad. Minh does not know how to handle Jaden. When I got home I said to my husband, "Why did you say that to our son?" Out of his mouth came nonsense. He said, "Because Jaden hit Hayden," or some other stupid excuse. I replied to him, "There is no excuse for you to say such a word to your son."

How can he say this to our young child? He is only eight! Little things we do and say as parents can hurt our children very much. Every day I say to my husband and my sons, "Think before you act or before you say something that might hurt others! Please!" I know that words and actions can never be taken back.

It is so important that my husband have a good relationship with his boys. I am thankful my husband likes to work; if he had to stay home too much, it would not be good for him or our family.

I know love comes in many forms. I am trying to hold hands, kiss, and say "I love you" more often to my husband. After giving birth to my sons, Minh and I did not sleep together in bed. This was a mistake. The love vanished, since I gave all the love I had to my two boys. It has been hard to rebuild that love. It is another important lesson I learned.

I learned my English from talking to clients and by asking questions when sometimes I struggle with certain English phrasing. They help me, especially when we talk together about parenting, marriage and other things.

In my life, I still have much to learn each day. I will continue to use my talents to create beautiful nails for my customers and make people feel good about themselves. I study all the time by watching YouTube videos and watching my best friend, Thanh, who is like a sister to me. They teach me different nail techniques.

I do not get any time alone, but I am looking forward to our family vacation this summer. We will go to Las Vegas with the boys. They love to swim in the pools with warm water. Last time we went to see shows like Shark Reef and explored the Titanic exhibit at the Luxor. Both of them love to sleep in hotels. Me, too!

CHAPTER TEN

Daniela

Daniela's spellbinding smile was the first thing I noticed. It appeared peaceful, yet pained. It was the first time we had met, and I was immediately impressed by how completely composed she was. Only twenty-two, Daniela has already faced many extreme experiences in her life. Her story can be seen in her soulful brown eyes.

Throughout her hometown of El Coyol, a small community of a thousand people located near Rivas, Nicaragua, she has earned her reputation as a brave young woman. With the help of Iain, a local Nicaraguan Spanish translator, Daniela articulated each aspect of her journey with poise and ease. It is obvious she is still making peace with her past and learning to let it go.

The vibrant sun was peeking through the palms onto the balcony near the Playa Colorado, a popular surf spot twenty minutes from Rivas. We discovered early into our conversation that both of us enjoyed Don Miguel Ruiz's book, The Four Agreements. *While his words impacted each of us differently, and at distinct stages of our lives, the themes of personal freedom and simple truths resonated with us both.*

Unveiling several layers of maturity to me, she stands apart from her peers as astute and empathetic. Reliving hardships is always difficult, yet she was willing to be transparent with me, exposing her personal pain on all fronts. Daniela recognizes how everything that has happened to her encouraged her evolution as a whole human being.

The time we planned to be together was not enough for me. I left her company wanting more—not of the white sandy beach and palm trees that kept the atmosphere light despite certain difficult subject matter, but of Daniela and her mood of gracious acceptance. As we parted ways, I mentioned how impactful her story will be to others.

Daniela is shaping her own reality, demonstrating self-mastery at an early age as a result of the demands life made on her in her two short decades. Living an intense life afforded her the opportunity to take damaging situations and find growth in the lesson sans instruction. I repeated several times to this extraordinary woman both during and after our interview, that she could be my life coach with her hard-earned wisdom and insight.

I did not fully understand that my mother was dying, but she knew.

"Ma" was what I affectionately called her. I was her youngest, and we were very close. She worked as a "housewife," cooking and cleaning for other families. It was a common occupation for many women living in rural areas of Nicaragua. My father was not around. I knew him, but we did not talk to each other. There was no love between us. He lived somewhere else, never getting to know my brother, my three sisters and me.

My heart will forever be hollow not having Ma here with me. There are still so many days when I just want a hug. Ma was only forty-years-old, and I was seven when she died of cancer. I don't remember many details of that time; I only recall seeing her lying in bed not feeling well. She fought so hard until the end. That is when she cried, not wanting to leave me and my siblings behind. One of my aunts told me when I was older that Ma had received religion in her heart, and felt complete when she passed away. I am grateful for that.

I will always remember a special passage in the Bible, from Joshua 1:9 that Ma used to read to me: "Have I not commanded you? Be strong and courageous. Do not be afraid; do not be discouraged, for the Lord your God will be with you wherever you go." I would read this verse over and over at times throughout my life. It always made me feel better when I was lonely and unhappy.

I know Ma and God are with me, but losing her at such a young age left an emptiness that I was never be able to fill.

My childhood was spent with my grandmother, Mita, who made *nacatamales* to sell. They are very much like tamales from Mexico, though nacatamales are wrapped in plantain leaves instead of corn husks. Mita would fill hers with pork, rice and potatoes. We also boil them, instead of steaming. I would sell them for ten *córdoba's* each.

My siblings and I all lived together with Mita, except for Jessica, the oldest, who had gone to Costa Rica when Ma became sick to work for a company that packaged *helechos* (ferns). She sent money to us to help pay for Ma's medical expenses, and later to help Mita support all of us. We were very poor, yet Mita did not always use the money my sister sent properly. I remember being hungry a lot as a child.

My grandmother did not know how to deal with Ma's death and she took it out on us. If I did not sell enough of the nacatamales, she would hit me with a small stick to motivate me. I thought she was a bad and evil woman, yet my work ethic comes from her. "I want you to be somebody in this life," she would tell me. Mita taught me how to survive on my own. By the time I was sixteen, I knew how to cook, clean and wash clothes. Although it was not easy growing up without a mother or a father, I knew I had to take care of myself.

On Fridays I did not have school and would go to my Uncle Jose Jesus' house to read books. My uncle was very smart and always very calm. He had many books; some were about education and self-growth that were very helpful to me growing up.

I was twelve when I first read *The Four Agreements*. What I remember reading is that children do not always make good choices. I could relate to this. Adults sometimes do or say bad things, too. As I matured, I began to understand and re-read different parts of Ruiz's book. It was nice to know that sometimes what adults say and do are not always right, nor do they know what is always best for me.

My uncle was very kind and at sixteen, I went to live with him. It was finally time for me to move out of Mita's house. I started to work in Rivas as a nanny to earn money. The first person to hire me had two children who were not well behaved; I did not enjoy this job at all.

Luckily, I had my Uncle Jose Jesus. I also had aunts and family friends, but I missed Ma. I wanted someone to talk to about difficult situations, and also someone to help me learn from my mistakes. I wanted someone to tell me what to do when terrible things happened. I wanted someone to support me, to tell me nice things, and to help me find my way. Mostly, I wanted love and attention.

In ninth grade, I met a girl named Dayana, and I felt like I had finally found what I was looking for. At the beginning of our time together, she made me feel safe and special. I could be vulnerable with her, and I told her all my feelings. Then people started talking about us.

Although I did not realize her intentions, I accepted that our relationship was different. I later learned she had been having intimate relationships with other girls before me. I was confused and could not fully understand my feelings, let alone what we were doing. We would kiss. She said she wanted to have sex with me, but many times I tried to tell her that I was connected to her emotionally, but not in a sexual or romantic way.

My Aunt Judith heard about Dayana's reputation and knew she was not a good influence on me. So my aunt and my family stopped our relationship. We were together less than a year, yet breaking up with her was like an emotional earthquake because I could no longer see or talk to her. The adults took my phone away because I was trying to text her too much. That was devastating for me.

They also sent me to a psychologist. I explained that she and I never had sex; we just kissed and held hands. Nevertheless, the counselor asked me so many questions! Do you like to paint your nails? Do you like boys? "Yes, I had a boyfriend in primary school," I told her. "And I like to do my hair and wear short skirts and pretty earrings." One time, the therapist asked me to draw the first thing that came to mind. I drew a boy. They were testing me to see if I was a lesbian.

In my mind I understood what was going on, but my emotions were still mixed up. I was really embarrassed. I knew I was not a lesbian or even bisexual, and I also knew it was not right to be with Dayana. I had just wanted attention from someone. I struggled with feelings of incredible loneliness. I had no one to love me the way I wanted to be loved. I was depressed. I felt empty. And I missed my Ma.

The psychologist helped me to understand how Dayana had taken advantage of my vulnerability. I also knew she had affected my life in a positive way, but many people will never understand that. I do not think of her as "bad." However, she completely understood what she was doing. I should not have let her take me into a world where I did not belong.

Shortly after that, I started classes at the local university learning to teach English as a foreign language. My hopes at the time were the highest. I had a stable job and I knew the basics of the English language. All went well until the expenses of the classes and my work schedule began to interfere. The professor kept asking me where my books were. I told him I did not have enough money to buy them, so I could not go on with my education anymore. This was really hard for me.

I continued to work as a nanny for a family from Mexico, who had two well-behaved children this time. We had fun together and the pay was good. My boss even taught me to make Mexican food. I enjoyed learning about their culture. They treated me like family, though I still wanted to finish my studies.

I was nineteen and felt free and ready to lose my virginity. I decided to have casual sex for the first time with a very handsome local boy. We met in a hostel; it was neither romantic nor enjoyable. I bled and did not understand why. He was older than I was, and had to explain to me why this happened. Feeling very sad, I realized that this was another thing that I would have liked my mother to have told me about instead.

A month later, I started to flirt with another boy named Jayquel, who was four years older than me. We lived in the same neighborhood. After four months of dating, we started living together. He made me feel special. We would hang out together, go to the beach, and hold hands. I felt butterflies in my stomach for the first time.

We fell in love. I wanted him to be my husband.

When I was twenty, I became pregnant. We were both happy and ready to start a family together. Jayquel came with me to the clinic. During the ultrasound the doctor got a concerned look on his face. He tried to explain that I did not have a fetus in my uterus.

I did not believe him. With my own eyes, I saw the fetus on the ultrasound. It looked like a bean. I told the doctor to look harder, but he told me again there was nothing alive inside me. Two more doctors came in and looked at the ultrasound. None of them were nice to me. I just remember there were many exams and lots of blood, again, like when I had sex the first time.

I felt scared and confused. The doctors were all saying different things. They thought I had cancer, and sent a sample of my blood to Managua for more testing. The results came back as a molar pregnancy [an abnormality of the placenta]. Then I was told the biopsy was negative, and that my pregnancy was normal, but it was too late. I believe it was medical negligence and malpractice on their part.

Yet what was I supposed to do? My baby was gone.

I felt devastated and depressed. It was an extremely difficult time for me. I could not stop crying. Second to losing my mother, it was my most painful experience. Why did these terrible things keep happening to me? Both my family and Jayquel tried to support me, but I was back to feeling alone and completely misunderstood. No one knew how to comfort me at the time. I wonder what Ma would have done, and what she would have said.

I would cry all day in my room while Jayquel was at work. He had an angry temper and was not always nice. Although he never hit me, he would yell and say bad words. Yet I still wanted to be with him despite his faults. I was in love with him! He was my life, and I was his.

Since I was still healing, we could not have sex, our relationship became stressed. He was with me, but he started to live like a single person. Then I found out that he had started texting other girls. I did not want to lose my boyfriend, but that emptiness in my heart was back, and I felt miserable.

We started to fight more and say whatever mean things would come into our minds. One night he pushed me down on the bed and told me, "If you go, do not come back." I knew I had to leave, but it was very hard. I remember thinking, I wish Ma were here to hug me and help me. I packed up all my belongings, left his house, and began living with my brother.

Only a week later, I found out Jayquel was dating another girl. Of course, I was still in love with him and felt very jealous. The girl would visit his house, and quickly she became pregnant. This was very, very painful for me. I was angry with my life again, but over time I realized I could heal my pain with help from my brothers and their children.

I learned that I can now live without my partner Jayquel, but at times I do not want to. We were together for three years, and it feels like it was for nothing. Ma would have told me, "You are stronger than you know and deserve to be treated better."

I have many unanswered questions for God. I know I am tired of feeling empty. It has been two years since the loss of my baby; I still struggle with that. There has been a lot of crying, but I always get up and go about my day. Every single detail and experience I have had has helped me to get stronger.

I found resilience. I can accept things that happen. I know that some of the people who come into my life make me feel good and some make me feel bad. For each problem I have, I try to look for a door, not a wall. My oldest sister thinks I am brave and tells me, "You are the same person, as if nothing bad has happened." I want to be a role model for others around me. I try never to say, *Why me?* even if I do not understand the situation.

One of my favorite memories of my mother is when we would sing together. It makes me smile. I can hear *Por Amor*, a Christian song about how beautiful a life is filled with love. I will always be wrapped in Ma's love. I treasure the time we had together. I miss her so much.

It is not easy to be calm and hold other perspectives during bad times. I have plans to go back to university and enroll in short-term studies. This would make me really happy.

There is a slang saying among the Nicaraguan people: *a mal tiempo, buena cara.* (One must try to put on a brave face.) I really work hard to be my best even though it is difficult and hurts sometimes. I am very proud of who I am, a twenty-two-year-old woman who has learned a lot from life already.

CHAPTER ELEVEN

Julie

I first met Julie while dining at a seaside eatery in Del Mar, where she has been a longtime server. I was immediately swept up by her spunky personality. She introduced me to the tender ribs, with honey sambal BBQ sauce, which I now order every time I am there. My husband and I, sticklers when it comes to customer service, were both impressed by how effortlessly Julie responded to everyone with her natural enthusiasm and charisma.

As our visits to the restaurant became more frequent, she started to share her story with me. Julie is a wife, a mother of two, and a cancer survivor. I was shocked to realize how much she had been through and what an unassuming warrior she was standing there before me. Her sheer strength triggered my own convictions: I refuse to give up. Julie had been diagnosed with stage-four non-Hodgkin's lymphoma T-cell, the same disease that took my own father when I was eleven years old. Hearing her story of survival, and sharing it here has been incredibly healing to me on many levels.

I always admire someone who looks adversity in the eye and says, "Bring it on—I'm up for the challenge!" This young woman is a living example of how perseverance and emotional strength are often just as important to the overall cure as the cutting-edge science reversing the disease. Julie never surrendered the idea of getting better, despite the unpredictability of endless testing and inconclusive diagnoses. She also never obsessed over the unfairness of being sick. She insists on learning to live through her pain without bitterness.

Julie went into battle with a dedicated support system of family and friends, especially her husband, Max. Hand in hand, hospital after hospital, they faced the struggle together. Max kept a blog throughout their journey. He sums up the situation perfectly in one of his posts: "Our life sucks right now, but it is not that bad; we are just on a journey and all journeys eventually end. We will come out of this on top and then we all can celebrate together."

My girls, Presley and Dylan, were six and three when I was officially diagnosed with cancer on February 11, 2013.

After the birth of my second daughter in 2010, I just never felt like myself. I thought maybe my body never fully recovered from the cesarean; I was always tired. Even simple activities seemed too hard. My husband and I had always been active, yet suddenly my body ached and felt depleted all the time. I still enjoyed running three times a week, but when I was finished, it felt like my lungs were burning. Throughout that time no matter how much sleep I got, I was worn out in the morning.

A simple bladder infection began my two-year journey discovering the source of my illness. I had pancytopenia, a shortage of all types of blood cells. The hematologist didn't detect anything unusual, and I was told that living with low blood counts might be my new normal. Iron and vitamin supplements were my daily companions.

However, this new normal still didn't feel right. At one point I had full-blown pneumonia, the bad kind, with fluid in both lungs. To make matters intolerable, both my girls ended up getting it too, and at the same time. A bronchoscopy showed inflammation in my lungs, but the root cause of my symptoms was not identifiable to any medical professional at this point. I was more than frustrated.

Six months later, my tongue went numb. Immediately, doctors ordered an MRI and found lesions on my cerebellum. I was in the hospital for eight days, which included a spinal tap and over seventy vials of blood drawn. Without a definitive diagnosis, the doctors suggested steroids: 1,000 mg a day for five days at a time. Maybe, they thought, I was suffering from multiple sclerosis.

Then my *face* was numb, and I felt like I was crawling out of my skin. Now I was getting used to not feeling well, but I was tired of being poked and prodded. I just wanted to know what I was up against; I needed answers.

Next, a CT scan showed "broken glass" in my lungs, which led to an open lung biopsy. The results were serious: cellular disfiguration, yet the specialists still couldn't pin it to a specific disease or infection.

Chito, an ICU nurse from the Philippines, was a breath of fresh air during my hospital stay. I vividly remember her asking me to remain positive and that she would pray for me. I was blessed by so many random acts of kindness throughout my entire medical adventure—and I am still thankful for every one of the individuals who brought kindheartedness into my life.

Another inconclusive MRI of my brain led to the first mention of lymphoma. However, without enough evidence for a full diagnosis, we decided to treat my illness as an auto-immune disease, with weekly doctor visits and even more frequent blood checks. Fevers were common for me during that time; every couple of weeks my high temperature would land me back in the hospital. Intravenous immunoglobulin therapy (IVIG) was introduced to help support my body's weakened immune system.

I tried so hard to maintain normalcy for my family. I didn't want to negatively affect the lives of everyone around me, so I did my best to appear healthy. I would waitress a five- or six-hour shift at the restaurant when I could, but that left me exhausted. Every time I came down with a fever or some sort of infection, it was a scramble to figure out how to care for my daughters, since Max was working full-time. My family and friends were our saving grace. Presley's preschool even held a bake sale to help financially support us. I was scared and emotionally drained; I tried not to think about what my illness could be.

Next up, I was advised I had an oversized spleen that had to be removed. The surgeons removed that organ through my C-section scar, which they informed me was the size of a small baby. Trying to keep things light, my husband and I joked that my body had delivered three babies now, not just two. Intense pain in my stomach led the doctors to also remove my inflamed gall bladder, which they sent to the Mayo Clinic for analysis. The result: lymphoma-like, but inconclusive.

Dealing with doctors, hospitals, tests, and treatments for over two years, I functioned on autopilot. In December 2012, while making dinner for the girls, I felt something like heartburn in my chest. So many weird things were always happening in my body, this didn't seem like anything out of the ordinary. Max was at work, so I didn't think to bother him about it. I went to bed and the next day took the girls to a dance recital.

Of course, that pain turned out to be a mild heart attack! It was evident now that my body was completely out of control. The swelling around my heart and an angiogram depicted a nodule on my left ventricle. I was confused and scared, and now I was taking heart medication, too.

Max always joked that I had a pill regimen like a seventy-year-old man. It was nice to laugh sometimes through all the uncertainty. What my husband did for me and our family was really an endless display of love, caring and support. He kept a blog the entire time I was ill to keep our family and friends up to date on what was going on with me. He was my devoted advocate and did such an incredible job playing the role of both parents when I couldn't be home.

I had started seeing a wonderful hematologist-oncologist who was willing to crack my medical mystery. Dr. Laurie Frakes left no stone unturned in her search for what was happening to me. In January, a squishy lump-like mass was found on the right side of my lower back. Dr. Adam Fear (which I always felt was a rather appropriate name) removed the mass. Dr. Fear was the same surgeon who had operated on my spleen and gall bladder—what was one more surgery?

Upon examination, the mass ended up being a nodule protruding through my skin. Oddly, part of me was relieved, not because the ping-pong size bulge was gone, but because the tests revealed the mass was malignant. I wasn't a hypochondriac; I wasn't imagining all these ailments. Something was wrong. I had learned to manage my daily life, despite the constant uncertainty. Yet now I was on a precarious edge. Finally knowing *what* was wrong might throw me over, but after two years of ambiguity I was ready for answers.

When Dr. Frakes told me to bring the whole family into her office on Monday, my stomach dropped. Part of me already knew what the grim news would be, and my doctor's face told me everything when we walked through the door. A PET scan, along with the test results on the mass Dr. Fear had removed, confirmed it. We had finally found what we had been searching for. I didn't completely understand the severity of why and how cancer cells spread and metastasize, but what I did see on the x-ray were so many tiny specks, I looked like a spotted leopard.

Non-Hodgkin's lymphoma rare T-cell cancer was not going to take me away from my family. Knowing what I was fighting gave me something to focus on. I had no time for a pity party. Deep inside me I could feel the instinct to survive getting stronger, and I knew I'd do whatever it took to ensure that I would be alive to raise Presley and Dylan with Max.

I can still remember holding Max's hand as we walked into City of Hope for the first time, the treatment center I had selected. I felt less lonely surrounded by people who were living the same cancer nightmare that I was. It was here I met Dr. Stephen Forman, an international expert in leukemia, lymphoma, and bone marrow transplantation. When he extended his hand and grabbed mine, it felt as if he was not going to let it go. He was such a gentle man. I walked out of the facility that day feeling literally infused with hope.

We returned to San Diego with a plan of action: a stem cell transplant. My brother ended up being only a half-match and I needed a full match. My name was put in the registry; we waited for the right donor. During this time we took family pictures and had a head shaving celebration at Violet's Salon. My Mom, husband, and girlfriends shared in the task of shearing off my long, dark brown mane. We made it a celebratory experience, involving Presley and Dylan; I didn't want my daughters to associate my baldness with being sick.

While we waited for a marrow donor, I went through four rounds of intense chemotherapy at Scripps Hospital closer to home. Let's be honest—chemotherapy sucks. Despite the illness, nausea, and hair loss I was determined to get my old life back. My girlfriends would take turns coming to visit and just sitting with me during the treatment. Their listening ears helped me cope with some very tough times.

One incident particularly stands out. Near the end of June, after dropping Dylan off at dance class, Presley and I walked down to Einstein Bagels for breakfast. I was wearing my usual outdoor uniform of workout clothes and "hat with hair attached." We walked down the stairs and into the bagel store—everything else was a blur. I only vaguely remember the kind lady who held my head after I threw up. I was told I passed out twice. This episode indicated to the doctors that I was worse than they expected. I ended up spending a full week at my "home away from home," Scripps Hospital, before being transferred to City of Hope in an ambulance.

The doses of complex chemotherapy I received upon my arrival were massive, due to my scheduled stem cell transplant. The high dosage treatments not only killed cancer cells, but also destroyed stem cells in the bone marrow.

Let me explain stem cell transplants as simply as possible: bone marrow is a spongy tissue inside our bones that makes blood cells. Bone marrow contains stem cells, and stem cells can turn into several other types of cells. The chemo had destroyed *all* my stem cells and they now needed to be replaced. Dr. Forman and his team took blood from a donor and substituted it into my body—my blood for the new blood, in a process called engraftment. Over time, new cells start to grow, making healthy blood cells. Before the transfusion, my blood type was A+. Afterwards, it was O+. I always found that interesting.

I hadn't felt great for years, but I never felt as bad as I did after the stem cell transplant. The bone pain was severe; I had to learn to walk again; my taste buds reverted to those of a baby; and I was brittle and weak from lying in bed. The procedure literally takes your body back to nothing and all you can do is wait for it to respond. Like a phoenix rising from its own ashes, my body had to revive itself.

My Mom took a leave of absence from work to take care of me. She decorated my private hospital room in a Hawaiian theme. If I was feeling strong enough, we would sit and sip a ginger green tea together in the cafeteria. I was on a very restricted diet: Cream of Wheat and Top Ramen were a treat! I wasn't allowed any fresh fruits or vegetables due to potential parasites. Mom would rub my legs after the infusions, which ended up being from a donor in Poland named Pawel. We had to wait thirty days, hoping that his stem cells would make their way into my bone marrow and start to produce new, healthy blood cells.

Max would visit every Tuesday and bring the girls on Saturdays. When I felt well enough, they would take turns wheeling me around in my wheelchair outside, on the hospital grounds. We would look at the fish in the meditation area or smell the roses in the garden. My daughters provided a necessary distraction from the pain, but not being home with them also added to the sadness and confusion that comes with cancer. I dreamt of our traditional family nights on Mondays, eating tacos and playing board games. That gave me strength to keep going.

One evening I passed out in the hospital room shower and woke up to my Mom sobbing. I had a fever and an infection. I was continuously vomiting and experiencing a horrific bloody discharge from my bowels. The physicians told me it was graft versus host disease, GVHD, meaning that my body (the host) was rejecting and reacting to the grafting. Pawel's donated stem cells saw my own body's cells as foreign and attacked them. The doctors said that experiencing a certain amount of GVHD was a positive sign because it indicated that the engraftment was working. Taking an immunosuppressant in small doses would trick my body into accepting the new, healthy cells.

Four-and-a-half months at City of Hope was grueling for me. I was taking twenty pills a day and having treatment after treatment from 8 AM until 4 PM every day. I knew I needed to go home for my soul and my sanity so that I could keep fighting. I negotiated a deal with Dr. Forman, a skill I had honed throughout my time at the City of Hope. Since the results of a recent biopsy showed that my body was taking to Pawel's stem cells, together we decided I could go home, but I would have frequent examinations with Dr. Frakes, take daily infusions of immune-suppressants, and continue to visit the City of Hope for bi-weekly check-ups.

I was not cancer free yet, but I was finally given the green light to go home two days before Thanksgiving! Mom and I drove to my house to surprise my beautiful, healthy girls. They were ecstatic to open the door and find me standing there. I presented them with my City of Hope "Champion" gold medal.

It was odd going to sleep in my own bed for the first time in months. It was also a huge change, going from a hospital room with just me and my Mom 24/7, to having Max, the girls, two dogs, a cat, and some lizards in my immediate environment. Of course, it felt fantastic to be home, but re-establishing myself into family life took time. My oldest daughter Presley would sleep with me; she didn't want me out of her sight. I remember taking showers alone, and literally sitting down to let the water hit my back. Although I was weak, staying in the shower and not having to face my new reality in every waking moment felt safe.

One year after leaving City of Hope, a PET scan and bone marrow biopsy confirmed that my body was officially 100% donor. I still have monthly check-ups and take immuno-suppressants, but today I am still cancer free!

When I was first diagnosed, I remember asking people not to feel sorry for me, but to fight with me instead. This disease was not going to be who I am; it was just another hurdle in my life to make me a stronger and better mother, wife, daughter, and friend. Cancer gave me a glimpse of death, but it also showed me a different side of life. For that I am grateful.

Suni

Listening to a live broadcast through Concert Window, Suni was introduced as an Argentinian singer, songwriter, poet and folklorist. This was my first initiation to this incredible woman; our interview was scheduled for one month later. I was captivated by the charm in her voice, and how she played her charango, *a small stringed instrument made out of the shell from the back of an armadillo. Suni had her listeners, myself included, engrossed in a Bolivian folk song, "Little Red Skirt."*

When I visited this cultured woman in her home outside Las Vegas, I anticipated her story would be about a vibrant and strong Latina performing in concerts to raise money for political prisoners in South America. To my surprise, her story was that, and much more. In between bites of egg salad finger sandwiches, we spoke about how her lyrics are deeply personal. While eating sliced fresh fruit, we discussed why her music propels emotions in men and women of all ages. The wooden watermelon napkin holders Suni used made me think of my Grandma Rosie and how she would set a well-dressed table for teatime with me when I would visit her in Michigan.

Suni is a source of endless energy. As a celebrated musician, she performed at countless venues including Madison Square Garden and Manhattan's famed Bottom Line. Her wandering life has taken her down many diverse paths. I was taken aback by and completely unaware of all her music credentials until she showed me a songwriting timeline her friend recently chronicled. The bold title read "Celebrating 30 Years of Songwriting." We briefly discussed her scoring of more than four hundred songs written and recorded for both children and adults. She has also published collections of short stories about growing up in Argentina and her early life in Chile. Suni was delighted to share with me that her most recent joy was in receiving an award for her autobiography, Destellos (Sparkles), *from the International Latino Book Awards in LA last September.*

Of all the many framed photographs throughout her home, one particularly stood out to me. Hanging in the hallway, an image of Suni in a striped dress leaning against a tree-trunk caught my eye. This portrait of a young woman playing her guitar under an enormous pepper tree reminded me of the importance of staying grounded. Sometimes we must trust life's process, even when we cannot fully see the outcome. Suni did, and still does.

Even now her purpose, passions and voice remain just as powerful as when she was in her twenties. She shared her love of language and cultural intelligence as both an educator and student when she came to the United States in 1965. When Suni revealed to me she was a woman of exile in her home country, having survived numerous vicissitudes in life, my focus shifted gears. After listening to her powerfully reminisce about the troubled times she experienced, I wanted her to tell me how she tapped into her potent strength of mind to overcome adversity and flourish.

Music has been her comforting chord, creating harmonic healing even when her life was unstable. Before I left Las Vegas, she shared a secret: "Never look back, only forward." I walked away that sweltering summer desert day recalling a distinct twinkle in her eye. Suni reminded me that miracles happen. They can also impart meaning and direction in our life, if only we are wise enough to listen.

I was lucky to be born into a talented Argentine-Italian-Catalan family of writers, musicians, linguists and poets. At the age of twelve, I started playing the guitar, writing songs, singing in choirs, and performing at family parties. By fourteen, I was learning Spanish dances and playing castanets. Yet I remember only one song performed at my home in front of visitors—a thrilling and scary experience.

It was Carlos' brilliance and musicality that drew me to him. I recall when my husband and I were young parents, we were both broke and jobless. Our first-born was not yet one. We were invited to oversee a relative's ranch, so we moved north to an Argentinian province, *Entre Rios* (Between Rivers) and found a way to make money and be together. Without any comforts to speak of, we stayed rent-free raising Angora rabbits. We fed ourselves by planting crops and living off the land. However, within a year, I contracted hepatitis from contaminated water. Very sick and near death, a local lady named Teresa nursed me back to health, while also caring for my child and refusing any pay. When I was well enough to travel again, Carlos and I left to find work in the neighboring country of Chile.

Even those hard, crazy times together did not prepare me for what was around the corner for us as a couple. From time to time there were signs and indications of Carlos' bizarre behavior; then he would ease back into normalcy. I recall one instance before we left for Chile we took a train ride to visit relatives in Buenos Aires. Carlos stood in between the wagons, shouting loud and clear that he was going to defy God and whatever obstacle was placed in his way.

During that time, I was shocked as I started to see the early stages of something abnormal in his actions. I let it pass and never thought that it might be an indication of a deranged or unbalanced mind. My eyes fill with tears thinking about our life and our shared common interests, particularly our intellectual conversations, our mutual love of melody, and deep respect for an exploration of other cultures in the world.

Unfolding right in front of me, my husband suddenly began to inhabit a world of his own—a world to which I had no access. It was his genius, according to the psychiatric hospital that took him away from me. With uncaring eyes, the doctors politely told me my beloved Carlos was mentally unstable and would remain suicidal, schizophrenic, and paranoiac, in an extreme dissociative state, living out the remainder of his life in a psychiatric hospital.

To this day, I am unsure of what triggered his mental breakdown. Eventually, he was removed from my reach and returned to Buenos Aires, Argentina. His uncle was a physician there and knew of a facility where Carlos could be kept in safe surroundings indefinitely. I never saw my husband again.

To tell the truth, I still have trouble absorbing what happened when I was told there was no hope of recovery for Carlos. Maybe if I had been wiser in the ways of the world or more knowledgeable about mental illness, I would have realized that something was amiss. Like my husband, I too entered into my own realm—a state of vast emptiness. All my emotions were closed up inside of me. I would not speak unless I was forced to answer. I truly did not know how I would continue living.

There was a law on the books in South America at the time, called *patria potestad,* "permission of the husband," which only allowed a woman to reenter Argentina with her children by her husband's consent. At the time of his illness, we had been in Chile for two years. Yet because of his mental condition, Carlos was unable to grant me permission for reentry. So, at twenty-eight I was stranded in Santiago, Chile, with our boys, ages two and four, with no job, no money, and no husband.

I had to consider myself a widow now, left alone to figure out how to buy food to feed my children and pay rent. I was having my own breakdown. Tears flowed constantly out of my sorrow-filled eyes and seemed to drown my traumatized heart. The doctor gave me calming pills. I contemplated taking my own life.

My Mamá, all too wise, gently reminded me, "Mothers remain with their children and take care of them." Yet I continued to feel a deep desire to sneak away into the dark abyss, in search of freedom from my despondency. With Mama's perceptive words echoing in my head, I slowly returned to reality. Then tiny miracles began to occur.

The owner of our house in Chile heard about my plight through the gossip grapevine. He told me there was too much sadness in my life now, so I should stay with my children in the house for free. I was not to pay him rent until I was established. My eyes well up with tears thinking about that tenderhearted Chilean man, whose name I cannot remember.

Times were still exceptionally tough for our little family. I never thought about myself, only about making a living. Money was scarce, and whatever foods I could buy or received went to the children. Needless to say, I was starving all the time. I had to give away our family dog; we had no money for one more mouth to feed. The neighbors a few doors down had been leaving food for our dog as a favor to us. I pretended we still had him, and I ate that food myself.

Looking for jobs with two babes in tow was a challenge until another miracle arrived at my door. Her name was Ruth. I remember opening to her knock at the door, and all I saw was her large smile and small red cheeks. She had come to the city from the countryside to make money. She and her family lived on the slopes of a volcano in southern Chile and survived after the lava spill from Villarica's volcano. They were in dire need as well. Ruth's help in taking care of my children allowed me to find a few miserable jobs and begin paying the bills.

My first crummy job was selling advertisements in the streets. I made a small commission peddling ads to every conceivable city business. After walking around all day, I would go to my other mind-numbing job at night answering phones for a dental organization. My third miracle was that selling advertising during the day paved the way for me to work at the best advertising firm in Santiago, Chile: McCann Erickson's Ad Agency. I was still depressed, however, and unsure that anything could bring me back to life, let alone awaken my artistic spirit. A more solid "way out" came in the form of an unexpected opportunity.

As I typed budgets at the ad agency, I quickly figured out that a data entry job bored me out of my mind. One day I took a risk by participating in a writing contest. A good friend encouraged me to enter, so I submitted my work and won! My creative fire was finally relit. Thank goodness for my DNA, those artistic ancestors who must have guided me through my time of doubt and despair. Consequently, I earned a position as a trainee copywriter, and advanced a few months later to begin writing jingles for the movie department.

It was with the addition of that job that I started making real money and paid my debt to my landlord, who had never actually expected to be paid. It took two years for me to make money "like a man," and begin feeding my boys and myself properly. Who could have imagined winning a writing contest with a fictional story about a woman and a mischief-maker monkey living together in the Chilean countryside would alter my life? Not me!

Little by little, I was slowly waking up and exiting the state of vast emptiness I had unwillingly and unconsciously entered when Carlos became ill. I began to notice the beauty of each day when I would walk the six blocks to catch the bus from my house to work. The mountains, sun and trees seemed vivid again, greeting me with their exuberance. It felt like I had been deeply asleep and was gradually being brought back to life again.

I took notice of the poor, lonely and desolate people in the streets and saw many children eating from garbage bins. This had been my fate for a brief time, and could be again if I allowed my misery to triumph. Through my grief, I understood what cracking my emotional equation meant: Accepting despair can easily equal continual suffering. I needed meaning in my life. I swore to myself, moving forward, I would make a difference in the world and do my best to change the ugliness, injustices and discrimination that I saw around me.

My two American neighbors were instrumental in helping me make extra money on the side. When they introduced me to a few Ph.D. candidates coming to Chile from the United States who needed someone to write translations for their dissertation research, I accepted their offer. These same resourceful neighbors managed to find me a contract with the University of Riverside, California working in the Latin American Studies Department.

Everybody knew America was founded upon the notion that everyone deserves the chance to shape his or her own destiny. I felt confident about my capabilities, and I wanted to explore my new identity, so I elected to move my family to the United States. It was evident I could further my schooling there, learning things that have always fascinated me. It seemed like the right choice, and an opportune time to create an even better life for myself and my two sons. So I decided on North America over my first choice, Australia. With Ruth's help, I closed my house, packed my belongings, and left for the new country with my sons, who were now eight and six.

Singing is how I always managed to survive, even if I was only silently singing in my mind. Music is part of the fabric of who I am. When song was not present in my life, I sensed I was retreating back to my state of gloom and grief. Exploring education in its many aspects, and accompanying it with musical instruments brought me back to living life to the fullest.

After getting a permit from the Board of Education in Los Angeles to sing without restrictions in the state of California, I started singing in elementary schools. I then furthered my personal study of music at the Polytechnic Institute. In my thirties, I applied to Douglass College in New Jersey, a part of Rutgers University. Yet after only a year as a music student at Douglass, the dean and the chair of the music department decided to solely focus on opera and opera singers. Since I was "too old" to become an opera singer, I was forced to leave the school and change my major.

Even with age discrimination, I was not going to let that prevent me from pursuing my passion. I forged ahead and transferred to Livingston College, and three years later received a BA degree in sociology and in Spanish literature. I continued studying and earned an MA in Hispano-American literature from Rutgers. In the interim, I continued to sing in countless venues, while also beginning to teach Women Studies in Spanish for the Puerto Rican Studies Department.

Now I look back at how life has a silly sense of humor. I recognize it does not pay to be upset about setbacks. After receiving my MA, I went on to teach in New York for many years, creating Spanish curriculums for music and language in both elementary and secondary education classrooms. During this time, I was privileged to begin writing melodies and lyrics for a few amazing women. The connecting thread throughout my life became teaching others about different cultures through music education.

Life can play pranks on us, yet its tricks taught me how to make a living and feed my children, especially during those five years in Chile. I will never forget my hunger, despair and abandonment. My past hardships and struggles have formed my many roles as an author, lyricist, singer, songwriter, recording artist, and performer of folksongs and children's songs. Each of those aspects offer me both healing and abundant pleasure.

I do believe being an immigrant to America fueled my intentions as a human being. My challenges allowed me to value my opportunities. My appreciation for education opened doors. I have always maintained a loving disposition for the essential human connection.

I never had the desire to be famous—to be the singer or songwriter of the century—but only to be the best version of me I can possibly be. If I am able to assure others that they too can survive deep emotional grief, whether through music, poetry, dance, or even creating melodies and rhythms for lyrics, then my overall life's objective has been accomplished.

CHAPTER THIRTEEN

Desiree

It was a predictably sunny day in Southern California. Desiree oozed effortless elegance in her white pants and summery tank top, sporting a string of mala beads dangling around her neck. She is an internationally recognized yoga teacher, with thirty years of practice under her flexible, form-fitting pants. Her degree, however, happens to be in dance, and she unquestionably has an organic way of dancing to the beat of her own soul.

I was immediately impressed with her transparency and passionate personality. I had been told by one of her students that she is a supportive and inspiring teacher, often incorporating real life stories and "kitchen table" wisdom into her classes and workshops. Understanding that life is short, she strives to live it to the fullest—a philosophy that inspired her recently released book, Fearless After Fifty: How to Thrive with Grace, Grit and Yoga.

Desiree survived a pain that no mother should ever know: the senseless murder of her twenty-year-old son. With patience and discipline, she came to understand that love is stronger than fear. This shining star embraced her grief and transformed her heartache, a lesson she now shares with others around the world.

Halfway through our interview, an enthusiastic admirer appeared at our table at a trendy rooftop café in La Jolla. The woman was visiting from the Midwest and recognized Desiree with her dark brown curly hair. This devoted yogini had taken her first workshop with Desiree thirteen years ago at the Shine Yoga Center in Cincinnati, Ohio. She just wanted to thank Desiree for being so compassionate and authentic at that time. Then she disappeared back into the restaurant crowd.

Desiree and I talked about how every heart shares the same hurts. She affirmed something I have worked to believe most of my life: that there is a way to mentally, emotionally, and physically transform the pain and suffering of our past. Desiree professes that the stages of grieving are different for everyone, and we are under no obligation to be the same people we were yesterday. To truly regain motivation and a sense of peace, we need others to help us combat our heartache, slowly re-emerging with a new perspective, full of love and gratitude.

I was teaching a weekend yoga workshop near Minneapolis. My son Brandon and I had been e-mailing back and forth, making plans to get together once I got home. At the end of the workshop, one of my students gave me a small book as a gift, *Ten Poems to Open Your Heart*. During the flight home, one very powerful poem entitled "Kindness" by Naomi Shihab Nye had an impact on me. It tenderly affirmed that, "Before you know kindness as the deepest thing inside, you must know sorrow as the other deepest thing."

Arriving back in Phoenix, I was greeted at Sky Harbor Airport by my father and two brothers. They were the ones to tell me that Brandon was dead.

My twenty-year-old son and his nineteen-year-old girlfriend Lisa had been shot to death while camping overnight, sleeping in the back of her mother's pickup truck in Bumble Bee, Arizona, about an hour north of Phoenix. They had planned this trip in celebration of their one-year anniversary.

When they didn't show up for work on Saturday morning, their friends knew something had to be wrong. Their bodies were discovered the following day by Brandon's best friend Tyler, who had been out searching for them. There was no robbery, no apparent motive. And even though the story was aired nationwide on CNN and America's Most Wanted, the assailant was never found. The 2003 murder case remains unsolved.

Brandon's father was the one who identified our son and he instructed the coroner to immediately cremate his body. It was probably best that I never saw him that way; my lasting images of Brandon would always be the beautiful, cherished ones in both my head and heart.

I felt insane knowing I would never see my child again. I could not wrap my mind around it. It did not make sense. My curious, creative, outgoing son was gone. Never again would I look into his brown eyes, or feel him towering over me with his muscular six-foot-three physique. I would never hug him again or hear him call me Mom.

The hurt was horrific, as if someone had cut me open and poured hot oil directly onto my heart. I wanted to be put in the grave with him. I had trouble getting out of bed in the morning, having to face yet another day without Brandon. Some nights I would pray that I would just not wake up the next morning. But of course, every day the sun would rise, and so I had to face my pain and grief. And I still had a teenage daughter who needed me.

I was in a strange state of mind. I was afraid that I would never feel any sort of relief, let alone joy again. I didn't want to leave the house, choosing instead to reside in a deep, dark hole with my sorrow.

People would say, "The pain will go away." In response, my blood would boil and I would silently scream back at them, "Where is the pain supposed to go?" Everyone holds his or her agony inside differently. It was only later that I learned that grief needs to move.

I started allowing myself to sob, scream, get angry, write in my journal, and talk about my feelings with friends who could handle it, or with my therapist. I bought twelve books on Amazon from various authors about how to live after losing a child. I wanted someone to tell me how to cope with the loss of my son.

I would search the shelves at Blockbuster for any movie with a sad ending, especially movies where people died. Tragic stories such as *Legends of the Fall* treated my sorrows like salve. If someone was being killed, I was completely absorbed in the content. It became an addiction; I wanted to feel all kinds of tragedy, not just my own.

My eighteen-year-old daughter Jessica lived with me for a year following Brandon's death. My adult children were extremely close, and they both worked together at the same gym as personal trainers. Together we struggled to process our devastation, yet often the pain was beyond our control. I was lucky to have her with me. We both had boyfriends at the time, but those relationships didn't last very long. Neither of our chosen partners could endure the grief we were experiencing.

Since Brandon's story was broadcast worldwide through different media outlets, strangers would reach out with random acts of kindness. Spontaneous flowers or notes helped me to know that I was not alone in my sorrow. I recall a man who walked into my yoga studio in Phoenix with a lovely plant as a gift for me; I had never met him before. He began telling me about his son, a Marine who was killed in the Iraq war. We had an immediate connection on so many levels. I shared with him how Brandon had joined the Marines when he turned eighteen, because he thought he needed more discipline in his life. He left the military shortly before the invasion of Iraq due to knee problems. I was so relieved at the time, knowing he would not go to war and be safe instead. Now in front of me stood this tenderhearted father who understood what I was dealing with: a type of anguish that lasted a lifetime.

I started reaching out to anyone with similar experiences. I only wanted to connect with individuals who had been through something horrific, or parents who had lost children themselves. My request was simple and always the same: Please tell me what to do. Coping with my sorrow was a journey I still didn't know how to take.

Even though I was in deep mourning, I continued to practice yoga. I remember being on my mat during an advanced practice and just collapsing into Child's Pose underneath a blanket. I rocked back and forth crying, while everyone else was chanting. I would sometimes dedicate the most challenging poses, such as Handstand to Brandon, imagining that he was holding me up. My heartbreak came through in the workshops I taught as well. I poured out my bleeding heart, while many of my students held my heart with me. I always remained vulnerable to receiving help from others when it was offered in a kind, generous way.

I was in so much emotional pain for those first two years after his death. I missed Brandon constantly. When he was very young he used to disappear and find our big box of dress-up clothes. Then he would suddenly reappear in some funny outfit, dressed like a clown, cheering us all up. Through the years, I had consistently been a joyful person, but without my funny and thoughtful boy, I started to believe my life would always have a tone of sorrow.

A documentary called *Fierce Grace*, about the life and teachings of Ram Dass began to slowly shift my thinking. As a New Age mystic and author of *Be Here Now* (1971), I had already found inspiration in his writings. My decision to watch the movie was to see how he handled his recent stroke and the repercussions. As it happened, there was a hidden gem tucked within the film that I felt was especially for me.

In the movie, Ram Dass talked about a couple he had counseled from Ashland, Oregon after their eleven-year-old daughter was murdered. I hit play, rewind, play, rewind, again and again. It was as if he was speaking directly to me. I clung to his simple yet profound words of wisdom about death. For the first time in years, I was actually comforted by his words. "For something in you dies when you bear the unbearable, and it is only in that dark night of the soul that you are prepared to see as God sees, and to love as God loves. Now is the time to let your grief find expression. No false strength. Our rational minds can never understand what has happened, but our hearts—if we keep them open to God—will find their own intuitive way."

The idea of infinite intelligence helped, but it was not enough to enjoy the holidays again, or to prevent me from becoming depressed around the anniversary of Brandon's death. I leaned very heavily on my spiritual counselor, Sharon. She "held my hand" on the phone and kept me off antidepressants with her gentle and powerful counsel. Sharon encouraged me to raise my vibration and meet Brandon soul-to-soul in the spirit realm. It took me several years to find that place, but eventually I was able to see my son as a soul with his own journey, separate from mine.

I was desperate for sustained relief, so in 2005 I decided to try *Panchakarma*, a purification ritual used in Ayurvedic medicine that intensively cleanses and restores balance to the body and mind. For one week I stayed in a yurt near the Rogue River in Oregon and had daily private sessions with a spiritual healer, Myrica Morningstar. When I told Myrica why I was there, she immediately laid down next to me in the yurt to contemplate my heartbreak and grief. When she opened her eyes, she had designed a personalized program to help heal my broken heart.

Her goal was to support me in gradually progressing through my bereavement. Every day Myrica offered different cures and cleansings. One form of healing therapy was a dough dam she formed in the shape of a heart directly on my chest. Tears and more tears flowed out as she slowly poured a hot oil with herbs into the heart-shaped vessel directly on top of my aching one.

On the last day of my stay, I had the most memorable four-handed massage. Myrica and her friend worked together on my right and left sides simultaneously. As they poured warm sesame oil on my body, they would not rub it in like an ordinary massage. Instead, it was sloughed off. At the end of the treatment, Myrica held the bucket of used oil in front of me and said, "This is your past, your sorrow. What would you like to do with it?" I opted to pour it into the Earth beneath the trees in the forest. I was making an offering; I was giving my son back to nature.

I treasure my memories of Brandon. I can hear him playing his many musical instruments—saxophone, tuba, and drums. He was so gifted; it seemed as though he could pick up any instrument and play it. I admire the sculptures and paintings from his childhood that I consider to be real art, not just the grade-school variety. I still cherish a gigantic 24 x 20 card he bought me one year for Mother's Day.

There is no normal grieving process. For me, the road was long, while I learned how to choose love over fear again and again. Little by little I began to understand that despair and pain did not have to hold me back. Other bereaved parents reassured me that in time, my piercing ache would soften. Over time, I would be able to return fully to my life again. Every passing year, fourteen in total so far, I look at Brandon's death differently. I am more dry-eyed, more composed, and more accepting.

During my many years of yoga practice, I have learned that it is possible to let go of things that stop me from being open to love and joy. This knowledge helped me be ready to meet my husband, Andrew, in 2006. Strangely enough, we had first encountered each other two years prior, when he attended one of my workshops in 2004, only six months after Brandon's death.

Andrew saw my rawness and tears that day. According to him, he fell in love with me instantly. He was attracted to me for who I was at one of the lowest points in my life. It gives me chills thinking about it. He has helped heal my heart and taught me to play like a child again. Together we travel full time, teaching yoga workshops and leading retreats all over the world.

I just recently reconnected with Tyler, Brandon's close friend of eleven years. They loved each other like brothers. He was the one who found the bodies of Brandon and Lisa; he still suffers trauma from the experience that day. Tyler was able to share his grief with me, and the devastating impact of losing his best friend. Sharing our woundedness has created a bond of understanding between us that I find quite precious and sacred.

I don't know what I would have done without my courageous daughter, Jessica, walking the journey of grief with me. Her personal healing took her to New York City for ten years. It was very difficult for me to trust in life with my only remaining child; having her so far away was an arduous adjustment. But during that decade, she was able to transform her sadness into a springboard for growth. I am so proud of her. She constantly inspires me with her strength and wisdom. She says she gets it from me, but I just shake my head.

After a few years, Jessica became interested in weight training again. Brandon had been coaching her, yet after he was killed she completely stopped. In a way, she went back to it in his honor. She is happily married now and runs an online business, *Live Lean TV* with her husband, who is also a fitness professional. They now live right across the street from me with their sixteen-month-old daughter, Kyla.

Every time my granddaughter and I play musical instruments together, I think about Brandon and his garage band.

Of course, Kyla is her own person and steps to the beat of her own little toy drum. But whenever we play and sing and dance together, part of my heart feels Brandon's spirit alive again in my sweet granddaughter.

Maybe you've heard this quote: "You've gotta dance like there's nobody watching, love like you'll never be hurt, sing like there's nobody listening, and live like its heaven on earth." That was Brandon! He lived his short, fearless life to the fullest. He will always be a blessing to me and my family.

Katrina

I sat down with Katrina in the living room of her cozy studio apartment in St. Catherine's, Ontario, Canada. Peering at us from across the room was a stone Buddha she had shipped back from Bali, where her most recent travel adventure began. A mixture of grapefruit and lemongrass essential oils permeated the air.

This young woman has an expansive spirit and welcoming smile. She was candid with me without hesitation, sharing her wild global adventures of the past decade. Our interview was actually a time for her to reflect on her gypsy ways and the courage and boldness it takes to be a young, single female traveling alone. To me, Katrina is the epitome of who I wanted to be at twenty-four. I enjoyed living vicariously through the vivid stories of her wanderings.

Katrina is a touchstone on many levels. I felt an intense and deep joy in being with her. As our conversation evolved, she offered a mature insight into what it is like to have been adopted as a child, in addition to how it was growing up with two moms and two dads. Like her travel itineraries, the relationships she has with both her biological father and mother (who live in different countries), and with the adoptive parents who raised her are unique.

She had prearranged for us to eat lunch at Treadwell, *a farm-to-table restaurant located in Niagara-on-the-Lake, which features world-class wines produced only minutes away. Since she was fifteen, Katrina has worked at that restaurant, and it is safe to say that this environment helped shape her self-reliance and work ethic.*

A sophisticated charcuterie board, like a culinary choose-your-own-adventure story, was the perfect pairing to our conversation. My last bite of roasted heirloom beets laced with a dill vinaigrette left me wanting more. I was also left wanting more of Katrina, a young woman grounded in reality but still curious about what the world has to offer. She is vibrant, adventurous and full of enthusiasm. I walked away from our interview understanding that wherever she goes, she goes with all her heart.

I was placed in a foster home two weeks after I was born, while the paperwork for my pending adoption was being worked out. My birth parents both worked at the horse racetrack in Fort Erie and were casually dating. It was my birth mom, Claudia's, decision to put me up for adoption. My birth father, Edward, found the adoption agent in St. Catherine's, and together they began searching for a family for me.

When considering the perfect parents to adopt and raise me, an advanced level of education was a crucial requirement for them. I have been told that both my birth parents were extremely picky in other necessary specifications as well, and declined everyone else until Nick and Heather, both in their forties, came along. Nick was a professor of political science at Brock University. Now he teaches communication and popular culture. Heather was a speech language pathologist and is now retired.

My mom, Heather, spent my early years reading up on how best to handle the complicated situation of raising an adopted child. She told me my life's story at bath time every night, about how I had been adopted when I was born.

Looking back, I had a wonderful childhood. When my parents were working, I enjoyed playing with Hot Wheels, riding my orange bike in the summer, or tobogganing and making snow forts in the winter. I never wanted for anything, except maybe more roast at dinner on Sundays. Both my Dad and I favored and fought over the lamb.

When I tell people I was adopted, many react with a reserved kind of "I'm so sorry" tone in their voices. Yet it's so completely the opposite! I often find myself saying almost apologetically, "No! My life has been the very best outcome any of us could have ever asked for." For me, being adopted never meant I was an unwanted child; it was simply that my birth parents loved me enough to want me growing up in the most supportive environment they could find.

During my teenage years, my Mom and I used to tag along when my Dad attended teaching conferences in North America. I remember visiting exciting places throughout Canada and the United States. Our travels to Cuba and Mexico are where I first encountered the difference between visiting a *resort* and visiting a *country*. My parents always juxtaposed resort life with village trips while we were away.

At the time, I didn't think it was cool or even exciting, but my parents would always take me on "educational excursions" that were off the beaten path. What I *really* remember was being at the resort one day, swimming in pools and eating exotic, lavishly prepared lunches, and the next day finding myself immersed in a local village watching cigars being made an hour's drive outside Havana, or staying in a canvas tent overnight in the Sahara desert, and waking up to roosters at 4 AM.

When we were traveling, I missed my friends back home, acting like a bratty teenager when I should have been enjoying the Sahara Desert in Morocco, or the national parks in Western Canada. Yet before I go any further, I need to apologize to my Mom, because during the ages of fourteen through sixteen, I said some terrible things and never listened to her. Picture the worst teenager—that was me. I remember once I racked up a healthy sized phone bill texting my boyfriend while we were on a family trip to Cozumel, Mexico. My Dad eventually made me pay the entire $400 charge out of my part-time wages!

At fifteen, with a telephone bill to pay, I was fortunate to find work through my dance teacher's husband, the sommelier and co-owner of Treadwell Restaurant. He gave me an opportunity to learn the principles of hard work and responsibility. Working part-time helped me shift out of my terrible teens, and the partying mode I was immersed in. The independence excited me, and I started making real money.

At sixteen, I did not want to have to ask to use the family car all the time. "If you want your own car, you have to earn one," my parents sternly stated. Since I was at the restaurant every Friday through Sunday, I often worked double shifts. Just one year later, I gave my parents almost $10,000 that I had saved from my paycheck and tips. A silver 2002 Jeep Liberty became my prized possession. It felt amazing to have my own wheels!

I dated that same boyfriend I had texted from our trip to Mexico for almost eight years, from the time I was fourteen. I learned to be independent when I was with him, since he was not very motivated—the complete opposite of me! Often though, this idle and inactive young man made me feel unworthy. He was very emotionally manipulative. I suspected he was cheating on me, but somehow he had a way of making *me* feel like I was crazy every time I suggested any dishonest behavior on his part. In my gut I knew. I stayed with him as long as I did mainly because I felt I could fix him. I see now that I should have left him sooner (we finally broke up when I was twenty-two), yet when I ended the relationship, I definitely recognized it was the right decision.

Thanks to my parents, traveling had always been such a huge part of my life ever since I was a child. But it wasn't until I journeyed on my own that I truly started learning about myself and other cultures. It was during my third year at University in St. Catherine's, that the desire to roam became bigger than me, quietly whispering in my ear, *"You need to be somewhere else."* My friends and family thought I was crazy when I opted to study in Hong Kong.

Hong Kong will always be a second home to me. The vibe that this city of over seven million people has is amazing! After having lived my entire life in St. Catherine's, a tight knit community of 130,000 people, it was the first place I really had to discover for myself. It felt so natural to be there.

I became part of a remarkable group with other exchange students. As friends, we would travel to neighboring countries, like Japan and Singapore, during breaks or long weekends. I took great pleasure being in an urban area one hour, and hiking on an island the next. I learned a lot about myself during this time. After having finished my studies in eight months at City University in Hong Kong, I decided to backpack alone through the rest of Southeast Asia. My parents were extremely supportive, although my mom said she did not sleep for the entire four months I was traveling by myself.

Bali, Indonesia with its warm hospitality was the very first country on my list. When I arrived, the humidity hit me like a wet blanket; the constant smell of incense was intoxicating. On every doorstep outside every house, families burned incense, and left food and trinkets for their departed ancestors.

Bali was also the first place I ever felt scared on my own when a man made advances toward me. The encounter with an Indian man was one of the first times I really questioned my instincts. That night I felt like the Universe hadn't been on my side. I wouldn't say I'm naive, but I rarely get that gut-wrenching feeling that I've made a terribly wrong choice. I've heard horror stories about traveling alone, and what to do to stay safe, but it wasn't until I was in the situation myself that I realized I could have been raped or seriously hurt, and nobody would have known where I was.

That experience taught me to take a few more precautions. I emailed my family with updates on my whereabouts, and learned how to fiercely throw a punch at a man if it was needed. I overcame those fears and left behind the idea that solo female backpacking is dangerous and unwise.

I also spent three weeks in Myanmar, formerly known as Burma. It was the only place in Southeast Asia where I didn't feel like I had to worry about getting scammed because of the color of my skin. When I visited, the country had only been open to tourism for a few short years, and locals just wanted to wave and chat with any passerby. It was and still is one of the most captivating countries I have had the pleasure of visiting.

In Bagan, Myanmar, I sat with a man named Yamin on top of a Buddhist stupa while the sun set. He told me all about karma and how we are born into this world with empty hands. We pass on to the next world the very same way, he explained. Yamin also reminded me that it doesn't matter what you have acquired throughout your lifetime, because you don't leave this life with any of it. What matters, he said, are the things you do in your life, for yourself and for others. I have carried Yamin's words with me since that evening under the stars.

Cambodia broke my heart and was a difficult place to visit without feeling really guilty. I experienced the absence of elderly people, since their generation was almost completely wiped out by genocide. Ho Chi Minh City in Vietnam is where I struggled with homesickness for the first time in my travels. A viral infection made me very nauseous, and I had to go into the hospital. All I wanted was my own bed and my Mom. I realized then that even adventurers need creature comforts sometimes! So I ended my backpacking adventure in Hanoi, the country's capital. I had been traveling alone for nearly three and a half months.

Arriving back in Canada was a complete culture shock. To this day, it is hard for me to enter back into reality after traveling abroad. People want to hear a five-minute version of my experience, something about my favorite country and the coolest thing I ate while I was away. Then the eye opening "Oh, you went alone…" comment arises. So I always have to gently explain I was never really alone; there were so many hostels and so many human beings in every country to offer me camaraderie and guidance that I wasn't "alone."

My fourth year at University was very busy and kept me out of the negative space I found myself in from being back home. I worked part-time back at Treadwell, and graduated first in my class, standing with honors in Business Communication. I immediately wanted to get my master's degree. I had mentally built my life around attending Simon

Fraser University in Vancouver, until they declined my application. That was a shock; it hadn't really occurred to me that I wouldn't get in. I was pretty heartbroken, although I came to learn that the Universe had other plans for me.

Feeling stuck and stagnant, when that urge to travel started whispering again it seemed like the rational thing to do. I was almost finished with my four-year degree when I went to the International Center and noticed a month-long volunteer opportunity in Namibia. This particular trip opened my eyes and ended up shaping my destiny for the next two years.

It was not the safaris, or visiting Big Daddy sand dunes that changed me; it was the desire to make an impact on the local communities. I felt passionate about what I had seen *not* happening in Africa with the volunteer program I was participating in. I was convinced the volunteer tourism industry was doing it wrong, and I wanted to make it right. The promo package was framed as a kids' after school program, and the idea was that we would help the children with schoolwork and also paint huts. Yet instead of facilitating and leading classes, some of my peers would hold babies and take selfies to showcase on their social media outlets.

I returned home from Africa in May 2015, and started my MA degree in Popular Culture at Brock University that September. However, my research was affiliated more toward Social Justice. I then wrote my major research paper, "For the Benefit of Whom? A Critical Analysis of the Claims of Volunteer Tourism," about breaking down the claims of what volunteer tourism actually does. I unearthed the fact that mostly young people typically go to places like Africa to increase their own self-esteem and CV resume, whereas their involvement should be centered on uplifting and strengthening the communities they had agreed to help support.

I can ramble on and on for hours about travel, exploration and adventure, because it is so undeniably worth it. Just yesterday I had a "memory" pop up on my Facebook page reminding me of my visit to Thailand. I was volunteering there, in Surin at an elephant sanctuary several years back. (This experience helped shape the way I looked at volunteer tourism, and impacted me greatly in writing my research paper.)

The village had two hundred elephants, yet only ten were part of the sanctuary project. *Mahouts* (elephant caretakers) were provided subsidized housing for assisting with the project, and were forbidden to use hooks or violence with their elephants. The philosophy behind the sanctuary was to educate locals from inside the village about treating the elephants more kindly. Instead of forcing the mahouts to think the way we do, the locals began to understand *why* the changes were put into place; then the behavior towards the elephants improved.

During that same visit, I also attended the Lantern Festival called *Loi Krathong* in Chiang Mai. It takes place on the evening of the full moon of the twelfth Thai lunar month, which typically falls in November. After the two-hour ceremony with blazing torches and incense and chanting, we lit small candles inside of huge paper lanterns; filled with hot air, we released the lanterns into the sky with our written wishes. I honestly did not have enough space to write everything on the lantern! It was the most magical experience of my life.

Here are my top two lessons I've learned while traveling, especially in the East. First, *things* will never make you feel full or happy. Some of the happiest people I have met have had very little in the way of material possessions. Second, spending time with people that matter the most is really important. As I have grown up, witnessing more misfortune makes me appreciate those who are dearest to me.

About a year ago, my biological father, Edward and I had a deeper than usual conversation during one of my visits to California where he currently lives. Over a late-night sushi meal, he became more vulnerable, and I got to know him at a different level. That same night he invited me to London to meet his mom and two brothers for the first time.

Ten months later as I flew to London, I distinctly remember thinking how bizarre life can be. I had recently learned that Edward was born in Newmarket, England. Coincidently, my adoptive father, Nick, was born near Folkestone, Kent. Only one hundred miles separated the two towns where the two significant men in my life grew up. I spent many summers in the south of England, in Brighton, where my dad would teach at the nearby university. It truly is a small world.

When I came home from that trip to England after meeting Edward's family, my Mom said to me, "This is the exact moment that I have hoped for ever since we adopted you." She told me that all she ever wanted was for me to have a connection with the people that had conceived me. That's pretty darn special, I thought. I realized once again that I am so lucky to have Nick and Heather as my Mom and Dad. They are so full of unconditional love and support.

There are not enough words to tell you how great my life has been because of those four adults. I may have a unique situation, but it means I have twice the amount of people rooting for me than most, and even more people all over the globe to call "family." I have distinct relationships with each of my parents; I am so lucky that each of them supports and encourages ongoing connections between us.

Honestly, I just feel so fortunate to have experienced what I have in such a short span of time. I can't wait for what the future holds. I live my life according to what makes me and others around me happy. I practice kindness with strangers, since you never know what story someone else is living. I'm mindful about my consumer purchases, because I know that there are millions of people who truly have nothing. And I chase every single dream I have, because what the hell is the point otherwise?

Adelaide

When Adelaide opened the box of See's Candies®, I saw her smile as she searched for the dark chocolate marzipan, but she ended up with a dark chocolate buttercream in her mouth. She grinned anyway. I realized there was profound symbolism in that moment. In life, we never know what's coming, but what's important is how we respond to whatever is happening.

Adelaide is an artistic young woman who knows how to capture a picture-perfect look in every room. We met at her beach bungalow. Her hideaway looks like a page out of Coastal Living Magazine, boasting seaside life mixed with unique vintage decor, and a few choice antique pieces tucked inside the cozy waterfront neighborhood cottage.

French doors opened to an indoor-outdoor living space, allowing salty ocean air to pervade the room. Adelaide advised me that she is a vegan, yet "I am addicted to chocolate," she confessed. "But never did I plan on living a life of addiction to alcohol," she casually continued. *The mild summer evening allowed us to nosh alfresco on quinoa, plantain, and black bean bowls on a table surrounded by assorted succulents in colorful decorative pots.*

After dinner, Dolce, her half-pug, fell asleep soundly on the cushy decorative pillows, snoring softly. I settled into the stately looking Louis XV armchair with lime green velvet fabric. Adelaide relaxed in the mustard seed-colored brocade French cane-backed chair.

What impresses me most about Adelaide is how she took her addictive destructiveness, mainly aimed at herself, came to terms with it and actually conquered it. She is now three years into healthy sobriety and delighting in life beyond her wildest dreams. Appreciating both her recently purchased mountain refuge and this quaint beach bungalow, she officially owns her past and chooses to transcend toxic environments.

As I was leaving, this bibliophile babe reminded me to take the dozen or so paperbacks she had prepared and stacked in a box for my Little Free Library. A favorite book of hers, especially during her recovery years was The Untethered Soul. *Adelaide explains the freedom she found in that little treasure, and how it taught her that she does not have to be defined by the opinions in her head. She has come to realize that she is not just her thoughts. Even if the voice in her head is a lunatic, she simply does not have to listen.*

Looking back, I remember wishing for a subtle manifestation or sign at the beginning of my recovery. I wanted some type of revelation or confirmation that I was on the right path and that all my efforts were useful. I was fraught with the concept of finding a Higher Power. As a long-time atheist, I just couldn't accept this belief that *something* greater than myself existed.

About ten days into my sobriety treatment program, I accepted that I was an alcoholic. I was still struggling with finding a Higher Power, but apparently having faith in something can be quite good for you. My counselor, Barney, gave me a few books and pamphlets to read about spirituality versus religion, since having a Higher Power in recovery is imperative. He told me I had to have something to pray to, to turn things over to, and to ask for help in returning to sanity.

However, I did not realize how much of a perfectionist I was until I had my "burning bush" moment. For me, there were no actual flames to accompany my revelation as in the Book of Exodus. My miraculous moment occurred sitting cliffside watching pelicans flying by, while waves crashed dramatically into the sea cliffs below me. The wind, clouds, sand, and sun were all behaving the way you would expect. Bathers were frolicking in the surf. Oh, and the sea lions were there as well. All of these elements played a role in that moment—my Joycean epiphany. As I looked out at the vast ocean with its imperfections and randomness, in addition to its extreme potential, something smacked me over the head.

I am not in control of anything.

No human being can ever command the ocean. And, just like that, I realized something else must be in control!

The Universe is in control, not "me." I can only control *my* behavior. I can only control *my* reaction to what the Universe sends me. I can't control people, situations, weather, oceans or pelicans. Life happens all around me whether I like it or not. I can only choose how I respond to it.

It sounds so simple, but it was literally the biggest relief of my life. I felt a gigantic weight lift off my shoulders and a freedom I cannot describe. I slept soundly that night for the first time in years, and I have continued to sleep soundly every night since. This epiphanic experience helped me find new meaning and purpose to my life.

I no longer get worked up when things don't go as planned. I try not to expect anything, since expectations lead to disappointments and resentments. I hope for the best, plan for the worst, and try to laugh it off no matter what happens. I no longer let failures or disappointments dictate my mood or behavior. I control my conduct and demeanor and am a much better person for it.

Booze was the magic that made me feel like I fit in, or at least diminished the feeling of being inferior and nervous around other people. In addition, I was not able to rock who I was, no matter who was around. It gave me courage— liquid courage—and numbed my greatest emotions: fear and self-consciousness. At various times in my life, drinking was a problem, sometimes more and sometimes less; but in hindsight the emptiness was always there. Being addicted to alcohol distorted my perception of myself, as well as the world around me.

Now when I am in a stressful situation, I rest in the faith that the Universe has my back, and that things will go exactly how they should. I try to learn from mistakes and move forward. I also freely forgive people, because I truly believe everyone is doing the very best that they can.

So, my Higher Power is the Universe or the spirit of the Universe. I might use the word God, but to me it's that infinite spark of the energy of the Universe. I believe the Universe has a divine plan for all of us, each and every day. Sometimes when I meditate I see a bright orb of light hovering over the ocean.

When the going gets tough, I just have faith that there is a lesson for me in what's happening. I don't always know why things occur in the moment, but the answers come eventually. I trust that now.

I envisioned Alcohol Anonymous (AA) as meetings of crusty old men with liquor bottles tucked in their pockets. How wrong I was! Individuals of every age, every walk of life, and every socioeconomic level were present. My treatment program was an eight-hour-a-day schedule that was based on a twelve-step recovery process using the principles of AA. The program was an important step in providing me a roadmap for life. My efforts provided immediate relief, and it was extremely important for me to be proactive in this process of recovery.

Basically, everything in AA is a suggestion; you aren't required to do anything that people tell you to do. Yet one of the suggestions is that you attend ninety meetings in your first ninety days. I think I attended about 170 meetings in my first ninety days. I really wanted release from the suffering of addiction and I wanted to do everything I could to get better right away. I recognized that the more meetings I attended, the better I felt.

Recovery taught me *everything* about myself. It taught me that I am freakin' awesome! It also taught me how to love others, even with their imperfections. It taught me that I can build a beautiful life for myself, and that I am literally the only person that I need in my life. I am so comfortable being alone now and still very social. Recovery taught me that I was living below my potential. It taught me I can do *anything* I put my mind to.

I was lucky to find my sponsor at my second meeting. She was instrumental in supporting me to nurture my self-worth and stop my horrible harmful patterns. I craved a non-judgmental space after years of trying to be perfect for my mother. This yogini radiated a loving, gentle and non-judgmental demeanor. Having her as a sponsor was useful to me in countless ways. She was an attractive, well-dressed woman who held a job and, like me, was a recovering alcoholic. It was then that I realized that anyone, anywhere could be an alcoholic.

Self-exploration was the biggest and most important part of the recovery process for me. I learned how to love myself for the first time in my life. Now, every time I am about to do something hard or uncomfortable, I remember, *I have done much harder things than this*. Recovery for me involved far more than just staying sober; it was about changing every aspect of my life. For eighteen months after finishing my treatment, I continued to attend meetings nearly every day. These gatherings became more about emotional sobriety, guiding me in practicing what I'd learned when difficult circumstances came up. They also offered additional support for challenging situations.

At this point in my life, there are always day-to-day struggles, like traffic jams, but truly, I don't feel like anything is a struggle anymore. Once I stopped my intake of alcohol, I had no desire to drink. After a few days, the haze cleared and the urge just went away. I am very unique in not craving alcohol, yet I also have learned to keep my mind occupied.

Reflecting back, as I have so many times, I was literally on the edge of a precipice. If I hadn't gotten the help I needed when I did, there would have been a fatal free fall. I never would have lived up to my full potential. Drinking myself to death was not part of my long-term plan, although that was what I was doing. However, I do believe alcoholism is engraved in my DNA; it is a part of who I am. It also might be useful to mention that both sides of my family tree are laced with this disease.

Throughout my life, my self-motivated attempts to be some kind of Barbie Band-Aid, endeavoring to keep everyone *else* happy and together, came at my own emotional expense. It was a heavy burden to carry, especially with my mom, who exhibited alcoholism and textbook narcissism all her life. Although no one fully understands the chemistry of addiction, from what I know now, dependence on alcohol and drugs can be nefarious.

I functioned at a high level from the age of eighteen until I was thirty-five. I convinced myself I did not have an alcohol problem. I could stop drinking for a month, but losing my tolerance during that time meant I only had to gain it back again. Alcohol gave me confidence, and I felt like I was fun to be around when I was drunk. My need to be perfect went away when I drank, as did the feeling of not being cute or smart enough. During my entire life, I longed to hear my mom say, "Just do the best you can." Yet those words never came out of her mouth. Unfortunately, that only ramped up my alcohol intake.

I took my first sip of beer when I was twelve. Although I disliked the taste, it did not stop me from stealing booze from my parent's liquor cabinet whenever I wanted. On my sixteenth birthday, I hid my handcrafted mixture of different distilled beverages in a 12 oz. Crystal Geyser water bottle and walked out of the house. During my college years and for years afterwards, sipping cherry Slurpees with vodka and smoking marijuana became my daily vitamins, just as Ecstasy was my euphoric supplement of choice.

Everything changed right before I turned thirty-six. I should not have been shocked when this guy with a fantastic ass and a tattoo on his chest that read "MOM" broke up with me out of the blue. It was a week before our scheduled trip to Hawaii together. He claimed I was too nice and caring for him to be with me—which pushed me over the edge.

From November until April, I drank myself nearly to death. These were the five darkest months when I literally withdrew from life, soothing my sorrows with eight to ten beers interlaced with four shots of vodka a day. The main thing I remember from that time is looking at myself in the mirror every morning saying, "I don't want to do this again," but then feeling so crappy that within an hour I was drinking again.

I actually mapped out where the cheapest place to purchase alcohol was in town. I would go into the store and buy toilet paper and a basket of other random stuff to disguise my alcoholic addiction. One time at a CVS Pharmacy, my hands were shaking like a schoolboy pinning on his first corsage, which made it impossible to punch in the PIN number for my debit card. The kind lady at the cash register did it for me.

I had no respite, except through having a drink. Soon, alcohol-related health problems began to appear. I puked. My fingernails peeled. My hair fell out. Alcohol thins the blood, and some days I looked as if someone had beaten me up. Bruises were like tattoos on my body. My stomach was a disaster. I had gastritis, an irritation of the stomach lining, from the absurd amount of alcohol I was consuming daily.

Inconsistent sleep patterns were common, and hallu-cinations—heck yes! One evening, my delirium involved a cop and an alien named Chet. Essentially, I called the police because there was a green furry fellow in my bed who was trying to talk to me. I explained to the tall officer that Chet would not leave; I had asked him multiple times to get out of my house. The officer did not defend me from the alien in my room. Instead, he asked me how much I had to drink and told me to go to sleep. A brain riddled with alcohol clearly cannot function properly.

Vodka was my venom at the end, since it never left a trace of odor on my breath. Even though I was living in a total haze, I agreed to fly to the Bay Area for my birthday to visit family and friends. That's when my last alcoholic blackout occurred.

Since it was my birthday weekend, I was supposed to be going to San Francisco to visit my sister, but I missed my flight on April 3 because I was a drunken mess. I rebooked for the next day, April 4, and drank while getting ready to leave. Thank goodness, Louie, my loyal cab driver, whom I often called to take me home after a drunken night, was the one taking me to the airport that fateful morning. He knew my circumstances, recognized my condition immediately, and called 911. The ambulance arrived quickly and took me to the hospital.

I later learned I had passed out waiting for Louie to arrive. A large period of time elapsed that I still cannot remember. I do recall waking up in the hospital and the doctor kicking me out without *any* resources or help. I took a cab from the hospital and began drinking immediately upon getting home, only to wake up on April 5 and begin my booze bender again. Later in the day, my sister knocked on the door and threw all the alcohol in my house away.

April 6 was the first day I did *not* drink. I count that as my sobriety birthday. Some people count the last day they drank, but I like to think of it as a rebirth. Had my sister not knocked on my door, I hate to think what would have happened. I am proud to say I am three years sober.

In AA, we call our sobriety date our birthday. We call our date of birth our belly button birthday. It's very common for sobriety birthdays and belly button birthdays to be close together. For me, April 6 is my sobriety birthday and April 3 is my belly button birthday.

Immeasurable times over those years, I looked at myself in the mirror and said out loud, "I am not doing this today." I wanted to stop drinking, but I couldn't. That is the insanity of alcoholism! Until I finally "handed it over" to the Universe, I never felt like I was enough. I thought my life would be boring and lame without alcohol. Yet it's completely the opposite. Once I stopped the cycle of drinking, I became free. I am more unrestricted and at peace than I ever imagined possible.

Work is no longer a chore; it's fun. I enjoy every minute of it. Each day brings new treasures, friends, connections and beauty. I do what stirs my soul: hot yoga, reading an intense novel, enjoying a meaningful conversation, or hiking with Dolce. Engaging in life makes me high. It feels great to be alive and I live every day to my highest potential. This is what living looks like!

Linda Lee

I first met Linda Lee through her talented life and business partner, Dave. Our husbands have worked with each other professionally for years. Dave is an incredible artist, as well as a marketing guru who helped me design my website for Living Legacies Ventura County, a project that brought women of all ages together in an intimate setting to share the wisdom of their life experiences with each other.

We were living in different cities at the time, but I still remember her husband saying, "You must meet my wife, Linda Lee. Both of you have a desire to give voice to the quiet, yet incredibly talented ladies that have advanced our communities and culture." However, I'd like to believe it was the great sense of humor, and the similar opinionated perspective of the two of us he was actually referring to.

Linda Lee and I eventually met on a double date with our spouses. In the lively atmosphere of the restaurant, she was a portrait of sophistication and classy elegance. I will never forget the slit-sleeved black short cape she wore, looking like it came straight out of a Paris boutique.

Sitting across from me, this woman's allure went beyond her intense intellect and intuitiveness. Our shared outlooks on life felt invigorating. Over the years after that first meeting, we continued to visit each other, deepening our connection. Linda Lee has always been so willing and comfortable divulging delicate information. This trait allowed me to really gain an insight into the depth of her grit.

Looking at this lovely lady, one would never guess at the trauma going on inside of her. She has been in and out of the hospital since her infancy, enduring seventeen major surgeries before she reached thirty-five. She has been treated for heart disease, mixed connective tissue disease, diabetes, and other related auto-immune disorders. Linda Lee is currently undergoing treatment for chronic diverticulitis and is awaiting bowel resection surgery, while also in watchful waiting for slow-growing adenocarcinoma insitu in both lungs.

I marvel at this lionhearted lady who somehow finds a way to balance work commitments and relationships, in addition to managing her countless physical symptoms and trips to the doctor. She understands the fine line between "living" with chronic illness, and "being alive" with chronic illness. I try to implement some of her genius and intuition into my own often off-balanced life. She is my inspiration.

Recently, she reminded me to simply slow down. I vividly recall her saying with a wink, "There is no step-by-step plan; living is a process of osmosis."

I was born nearsighted, pigeon-toed, with a club foot and scoliosis. And that was only the beginning! Pain has been my lifelong companion; I've never known life any other way.

My family struggled financially since Dad was disabled and could not work. He was an angry man. There was never respect between us, yet I did feel sorry for him and his ill health. I know that he loved us, but any form of affection from him was nonexistent. I felt a sort of emptiness inside, especially when he was alive.

My mom was the one who supported me. She boosted my confidence and encouraged me to cultivate my mind. I wish she had not allowed herself to be held hostage by my father's disability and tantrums, which more than likely prevented her from leaving the marriage, along with aiding her sense of dependency. He had severe heart disease, but his psychological abuse towards her was incredibly destructive. I often got caught in the crossfire; that dynamic has adversely affected me in many ways.

My childhood traumas made me realize two things: first, I had to find a way to support myself; second, I did not want to be like my parents. Over the years I learned how to be different, and rise above those negative habit patterns.

During my early years, I was simultaneously smart and rebellious, so I managed to steer clear of the toxic environment at home. When I was eleven, I got a job cleaning our neighbor's house, four days a week. By thirteen, with a heavy dose of make-up to look more mature, I worked at Don Ricardo's Mexican Restaurant as a hostess, working forty-hours a week, while still going to school.

My hard work paid off at sixteen when I purchased my own car. Not having to ride the bus to and from work wearing my long green wraparound skirt, and the ruffle blouse with multicolored embroidery was a huge step toward the freedom I longed for. As a voracious reader, I had the insatiable desire to wander the world and escape my stifling environment.

I will never forget Daniel Fernandez, the handsome bus-boy with piercing blue eyes, who also worked at the restaurant. A journalist in his late twenties, he was exiled from Argentina for writing against Eva Peron. The stories he shared about his own hardships made me think about my life differently. I realized that my own struggles could be an opportunity to work, to learn, and to advance myself.

Against my father's wishes, I used my earnings from work and traveled to Chile with a group of teens and the "Youth for Understanding" organization. In college, two years later, I was studying in Spain. However, intense side effects from "female problems" that began early for me around the age of twelve, interfered with these new adventures abroad. Regrettably, I did not finish my degree in Madrid due to cervical dysplasia. I had to return home for cryosurgery, a procedure that involved using extreme cold to destroy abnormal tissue. I was eighteen.

During the next seven years, pain and constant bleeding were my companions, as I underwent four laparoscopic proce- dures for ruptured cysts and fibroids.

Somehow, I managed to graduate from California State, Northridge with a degree in Spanish literature. While working in the international department at the Bank of America handling foreign currency, I was living in a barn turned studio. All during this time I kept feeling that I was "due" for something positive in my life.

Sure enough, one bright sunny day, into the bank walked Walter Harvey Evans, a gentleman who worked at the local State Farm Insurance Agency. After complimenting my fluent Spanish, he asked if I wanted to work for him, explaining I would not be selling insurance, only speaking Spanish and handling reservations for fishing resorts in Baja, Mexico. He also said, "I'll double your salary, whatever it is." It felt like a risk, yet it was a decision that had many unforeseen and positive influences in my life. *Adios*, barn; hello, new apartment!

One of my frequent clients at that time became my first husband. He was twenty-six years older than me, and he swept me off my feet with his fanciful life and wealthy inclination. I was ready to settle down and start a family with this man. Since we talked extensively about having a baby together despite my ongoing health concerns, we visited a specialist at Scripps Hospital. Unfortunately, it turned out that he had been making similar plans with my college roommate from Spain. We divorced. Shortly, afterwards my gallbladder ruptured. It was the luck of the draw, losing both my husband and my gallbladder at the same time. Strangely enough, it was my gallbladder of twenty-seven years I would miss the most.

Time allowed me to slowly gain back my self-reliance. I still longed for a family and children, but the idea of both of those were put on the back burner. In the meantime, I was diagnosed with interstitial cystitis, a type of inflammation with symptoms that often mimic bladder cancer. I had severe pelvic pain and pressure, with a frequent urge to urinate. Yet I continued to work and travel while treating this condition with DMSO, a liquid medication administered through a temporary catheter.

Without much guidance in my life from any mentor, I was not particularly career savvy or even career oriented. I spent my life in search of easy money to support myself, in addition to taking opportunities that easily presented themselves. I did not plan ahead, other than for receiving my BA degree. I did not pursue passions other than those of the flesh. Instead I pursued money and health insurance.

So when an opportunity came along for me to start my own marketing and reservation company in the big game and fishing industry, I was elated, albeit a bit anxious. I was approached by two self-made American businessmen who had built a hotel in Baja in a remote area on a peninsula surrounded by the Sea of Cortez. Their forty ocean front suites were located in the best fishing grounds in Mexico. Realistically, these men knew nothing about fishing, nothing about Mexico, or the vertical market they had entered. I was now an expert in this area due to my association with Walter Harvey Evans. The men had heard I was trustworthy, knew what to look for, and knew how to get things done.

I was twenty-eight when South of the Border Enterprises, my own marketing and reservation company was born. I worked non-stop. I was soon the representative and marketing liaison for seven hotels, traveling extensively back and forth to Mexico. My life felt like a circus act, constantly juggling and then continuing to juggle as another ball was tossed into the mix I was attempting to keep aloft. Although I didn't have time for Fibromyalgia and Chronic Fatigue Syndrome, or the accompanying loss of concentration, along with unexplained muscle pain, I dealt with it. During this time, the most frustrating part was that the fatigue, of course, worsened with activity, but did not improve with rest. So I became more tired every day.

I went through life with a mask on. It was crucial for my livelihood that I keep my symptoms and high level of stress in check. If either my bosses or clients knew how sick I was, it may have prevented me from getting jobs and associated benefits.

Trying to disguise my body and outward appearance became a main priority; my secondary priority was making enough money to cover my pricey medical expenses. I needed to look healthy, cute, and chic so no one would see how unhealthy and depleted of energy I really was.

Many people presumed make-up and stylish clothes were significant parts of my delights. I allowed them to see me like a character in a movie, rather than reveal my true identity. The further I concealed my role, the more I became a personality that was not reflective of who I truly was. At the time, I was too self-doubting and defensive to recognize what

I was doing. Sadly, I went overboard, and the act became extremely exhausting.

I was a one-woman show, selling and servicing for seven hotels, as well as marketing on a consulting basis. Eventually, I had to hire a couple of employees to help me. By that time I was also designing the hotels' marketing, sales, and media plans, which included traveling to trade shows, which was an enjoyable addition that took my mind off my ailments. To this day, I pride myself in being an early adopter of new tactics and technology. In fact, I had one of the first computerized reservation systems for hotels.

It was not uncommon to be surrounded by men due to my line of work. I ended up engaged, twice. Both were a bust. Neither man understood the severity of my sicknesses, nor did they treat me with any compassion whatsoever. Yet it was a fun distraction living on a boat in Sausalito for six months with my techie fiancé. The other short-lived love interest was an Australian fishing entrepreneur.

I suppose in retrospect the "passions of the flesh" could have been a craving for intimacy of any kind, and the affection I never received as a child. Over decades, I managed to get involved in an endless stream of bad relationships in search of love, endearment, closeness and stability.

By the time I was thirty-three, my lifestyle was catching up with me. Going from one disease to another, one fiancé to another, one fishing property to another came with a heavy price. While my business unraveled, I met my current husband, Dave, and we dated on and off. I was living in Orange County and he was in San Diego. We were working on a hotel project located in the seafront city of La Paz, Mexico. A hefty lawsuit from one of my travel bookings brought enormous stress, lawyer bills, and finally the closing my business of twelve years. I was overwhelmed.

It was in the midst of this chaos that Dave and I attempted fertility treatments together, a last-ditch effort with artificial insemination. We knew there was no guarantee I would conceive due to all my health issues. I knew the risks, but did not want that feeling of regret for not trying. The exacerbation of my bleeding, interstitial cystitis, and extreme pain and anemia led doctors to determine a hysterectomy was needed. That was when my hope of conception ended.

You would think by this time I would have known how to address and cope with the pandemonium in both my personal and professional life. With Dave, my outlook did begin to change, so that eventually pushing my personal and professional parameters to extremes came to a grinding halt.

With great pride I can say my supportive partner and I continue to thrive after twenty-five years of working together in sales and hotel marketing. Right now, he struggles with his own health matters. In fact, we swap medical stories, laughing in bed together recuperating. "Well, we have each other," is our motto, which helps us keep it humorous.

In consecutive years, being told I had diabetes, as well as a mixed connective tissue disease was almost devastating. In fact, it took such a toll that I had a heart attack three years later. Two stents are keeping me alive. I recognized then that it was time to focus my attention on my health, forgoing the frantic work pace I had set for myself for so many years. Sadly, in the midst of that, my sister underwent quadruple heart surgery, yet subsequently died. I could not attend her funeral due to my own recuperation.

On a daily basis, many women run on "fumes," rarely having the luxury of filling their "tank." I like to think I have a serene sensibility about me, but for some odd reason it always took a tragic event, a life-threatening disease, or a death to reset my mode of thinking. Maybe it's because I'm stubborn, or we live in a society where our self-esteem is tied up in the work we do to make a living. Either way, I became a compulsive achiever, often letting nothing stand in the way of making my career, family status, and accomplishments *highly successful*. This way of thinking and living left me empty.

When they found cancer in both lungs, the doctor told me to assume I had five years to live. Then he asked if I was prepared to die. I realized it was finally time to seek the help of a psychologist. Therapy helped me acknowledge my talent of hiding my feelings all those years. I began the journey of taking my life in a different direction. I allowed my mask to completely fall off. I reduced my workload to only two accounts. I detached myself from my old measurements of success.

Fine-tuning and rethinking my priorities was lifesaving. I now avoid stress and conflict at all costs. I focus on what I want to do and what brings me happiness. We recently adopted our lovable dog, Coco, a Coton de Tuléar, and considered canine royalty. Dave and I felt it appropriate to borrow Coco Chanel's name for her. Coco and I eat peanut butter frozen yogurt together. She keeps my spirits up, forcing me to focus on something besides myself.

These last four years have been the *first* four years of my life where I literally have had no control over my destiny. I am three and a half years into stage four slow growing cancer in both lungs, all lobes. I have not wanted to know the actual sizes and details. I am waiting to become symptomatic before I start treatment, which will impact the quality of my life until I die.

I wake up every day and take stock of my fatigue, stomach pain, chest pain, and everything else. Once I determine the extent of it all, I figure out my best plan of attack for the next few hours. I treat my symptoms with whatever pill, salve, herbal supplement, or tonic—okay, joke about it—then move on the best I can.

I have recently returned to denying my illnesses in favor of jumping into client issues, projects pertaining to Dave, Coco, friends or family. It would be super easy to slap a defect sticker on myself, and lay down and cry in the corner. But I have learned to cope and make peace with my chronic illnesses.

Tristen

I find myself enjoying the peaceful aromatic lobby of Mission Oaks Counseling and Wellness Center. The soft music and dimmed lights draw me into a mindful, yet expansive state. A larger-than-life copper oak tree projects from a water feature, delighting my visual sense, as the soothing sound of trickling water fills the space. A familiarity within this atrium emotionally impacts me from previous formal appointments, but today I am visiting to discuss the life story of my dear friend and confidante, Tristen.

Our history goes back ten-plus years, as it was she who guided me through tumultuous times in my own life with her practical advice. With compassion, insight and support, Tristen provided a sacred space for me to clear my mental turbulence. For more than a decade, she has always stressed to me the importance of listening to my heart, while working diligently to achieve my goals.

I happened to be back in Ventura County where I once lived, but only for the day, which made coordinating our time together a bit challenging. Time is certainly both precious and finite for each of us. In addition to wrangling two charming toddlers and owning a thriving wellness business, Tristen is an active member of her community, serving on various medical panels and presenting talks on topics such as "Raising Teenagers" and "Balancing Stress Management for the Family." Useful information, to be sure.

I've brought unsweetened black iced tea and cream cheese brownies from a favorite local café for us to share. I take a seat and wait for our "session" to begin. The thought of her tousled blonde hair, infectious laugh, and strong vibrant presence makes me smile. She can sometimes appear to be a contradiction to the blissful surroundings of the wellness center. "Give yourself permission to do what makes you f-ing happy," was her common counsel to me years ago.

Tristen teaches by example. We share obsessive-compulsive tendencies, which take our conversations down many paths, but somehow we always seem to come back to the puzzle of parenting. Over time, we have compared meticulous mental notes in a combined effort to perfectly harmonize our overextended lives and dysfunctional family dynamics. Seeing her again reminds me to pay attention and live a life that feels right to me, not one that looks right to everyone else.

My mother is the sweetest person on the planet, and Mommy is who she will always be to me. Doting and adoring, ceaselessly surrounding me with unconditional love even when the diarrhea of my mouth and lack of focus got me in trouble, she is my all-time supporter.

As my Permanent Chief Executive Consoler, Mommy bolstered me when I was growing up and was having trouble making new friends, feeling like an outsider. She imparted her love for the beach and books by taking me and my siblings along to her favorite locales. This distraction never failed to ease my discontent.

In school, books of all kinds engaged me when teachers could not. I would escape with the complex characters I read about, and we'd become fast friends. Countless novels helped shape my early thinking. Significantly, Alice Walker's *The Color Purple* left an imprint on my young mind. At twelve, this Pulitzer Prize-winning novel taught me how life can go from bad to worse; yet having perseverance, while holding on to one's dreams can be life-changing. I remember thinking if I could *read* about incredible abuse and bigotry, then I would be able to handle difficult circumstances in my own life.

Grasping concepts came easily to me, and all too often, I was bored and disengaged from reality and what swirled around me in life. Struggling to sit still and listen was problematic, in conjunction with a desire to be involved in the world "my way." These patterns forced me regularly into school detention. I was an extremely curious child (with more than a hint of stubbornness) and certainly not compliant.

My preoccupied father was never sure how to handle me when I was growing up. As a Certified Public Account turned Business Consultant, with his many titles of President, CEO, CFO and COO, we moved many times. It didn't take me long to figure out how to function as I wanted and not be affected by my dad's prickly parenting style. I often challenged his overbearing demands. I vividly remember the time in middle school when I defied him and began calling him by his first name, Lane. I had outgrown his standard strategy of "because I said so," deciding there was no longer a need to refer to him as Dad or Father anymore.

Mommy took time to understand me; Lane did not. He was not warm and fuzzy. He did not coddle my youthful sensitivities, and he never gave off a dad vibe to me. The more demanding and controlling he attempted to be, the less influence he had over me. His parental intrusiveness forced me to do whatever had an opposite effect. I was a classic defiant teenager.

Typically, during high school, my friends would drive me to school since I was the youngest in the group, and I willingly preferred to ride with them. It was always a nightmare being trapped in the car with Lane, whose main hobby in life was to lecture me.

I remember it was the fall semester of my junior year. With leftover liveliness from my September birthday, and having just turned sixteen, I was excited to be enrolled in AP Psychology. My deeply devoted mother and my strained father/daughter dyad was the incentive for me to begin analyzing human behavior. That morning was one of those rare occurrences when I was a passenger in Lane's car. Driving in the blue Chrysler minivan, I was jabbering about how much I enjoyed my psychology class, learning about the brain and the way people process information. Near the end of my speech, I proudly declared how I could really see myself pursuing a career in the help and healing profession.

When Lane stopped in front of the school to let me out, he sternly proclaimed, "You can't pursue psychology. That's crap! You'll never make any money doing that. You need to go into business." I was not trying to be a little shit, but I was flabbergasted, and completely disagreed with him. Taking a moment, I thought about what he had said and shrewdly replied, "Well, I think I can do both!" Walking into school feeling more drawn to and committed than ever to pursue psychology, I was floating five feet off the ground.

This particular conversation was a crucial moment for me, although I did not understand it at the time. I would eventually live my way into my own answer, with or maybe without knowing it. My father's reply most likely unconsciously motivated me, yet it definitely empowered me to pursue my passion.

I went on to graduate from the University of Utah with a degree in sociology and criminal justice. I thought that perhaps working with the FBI would be my career choice. I was fascinated by interesting accounts my paternal grandfather would regale us with from his times as a Captain in the Albuquerque Police Department. Growing up, his stirring stories kept my attention when not much else could. However, it was the requirement that I speak two languages that precluded me from pursuing a career path with the FBI.

Just as I began my graduate studies, my husband at the time decided he would be relocating for a significant promotion. The ultimatum came as he threatened divorce if I did not prioritize his dreams over mine. This was a big "aha" moment; I knew then that this marriage was over.

When I elicited the help of a marriage and family therapist, I realized I was working through layers of childhood wounds. I had been trying to sort out my relationship with my dad by marrying someone similar to him. My husband was definitely the wrong guy for me, not only in the addictive and aggressive way, but in the controlling, narcissistic, moody, and emotionally abusive way of my father.

I acknowledged then I did not need permission to pursue my dreams from any man, most of all from Lane. My four years of dysfunctional marriage taught me a lot about healthy and unhealthy boundaries. I began to learn how to assert myself in useful ways. I walked away single, with only Tyson, my loyal and brave boxer as a companion. That canine's caring and compassionate personality was therapeutic not only for me, but also for my future adolescent clients. He related to their mischievousness one hundred percent!

As I reflect back, when I sat at a picnic table with my parents and confessed that my marriage was over, citing irreconcilable differences, it was really the first time they saw my hurt, fear and sincerity. I shared the anger, addiction and abuse that went on for me during that time. I explained how I was afraid to stay in the marriage, let alone conceive children with this man. That moment of vulnerability might have been the tipping point when our daughter/dad dynamic started to shift into a more healing direction.

I quickly found restoration through my work at Casa Pacifica, a shelter for abused and neglected children. They were my family for eight years; this is also where I met the future father of my children, Cameron. He and I complement each other, although not in the cheesy, "You complete me" way from the Jerry Maguire movie. For both of us, it was important to co-parent and nurture an emotionally intelligent family together.

As Program Manager at Casa Pacifica, it was challenging yet rewarding to design, develop and train supervised teams for a one-to-one behavioral coaching program I had implemented. What was really cool was that this program turned into a state mandated health service known as Therapeutic Behavioral Services. A feather in my cap, for sure!

My involvement with the management team offered additional insight and information that I would later use in my solo career, as did working in the counseling clinic assisting numerous at-risk youth and their families. It became clear I actually could do both business *and* psychology as I had foreseen decades before; knowing this led me further into pursuing my personal path. This realization also propelled me back to school to obtain my master's degree in psychology, with a minor in shitty student loans.

This last comment made me remember something funny. My loving, handsome husband reminded me the other day how it makes him laugh when I lapse into my "trucker mouth outbursts." He jokes that I have the capability of slinging a cuss word into sentences like no one he's ever seen.

It is rare that I actually become upset and angry, which makes it comical to him when I use random profanity. By far, the f-word is my favorite, with *shit* being a close second. The fact that Cameron marvels about my masterful ability to combine cuss words in a way no SWAT officer even comes close to, is an enormous compliment.

Sorry to get off topic. Occasionally, I tend to do that.

When I graduated, I had an MA in psychology, with an emphasis in marriage and family therapy. Yet I was at a crossroad of choices for my career. A job offer to take over an established private practice for a clinical psychologist whom I deeply respected presented itself. However, my now-former clinical supervisor and eventual business partner, Michelle, harmonized with my thoughts on how we could expand the scope of healing in this domain. I was ready to prove that combining the world of business and the realm of psychology was attainable.

Even though Michelle and I are eleven years apart in age, we joke about sharing a brain. Both of us are nurturers who work hard and rest in autonomy. She helped me see my future by modeling it. She epitomized how as women, we can have it all—career, healthy marriage, and closeness with our children. It all circled back to setting appropriate boundaries.

We had many heartfelt talks, with more than a few strategizing sessions; we finally decided it was time to take a leap of faith, journeying together toward our collective aspirations. Her assertiveness and drive, coupled with her wholehearted compassion, intelligence and keen intuition, matched the qualities of mind and character that were important to me.

We found an ideal space to rent, and designed the Mission Oaks Counseling and Wellness Center (MOCWC) to embody our visions. It was imperative that our philosophy encompassed all layers and aspects of a person: psychological, physical, spiritual, social, and intellectual, ensuring overall wellness and vitality. Our center has numerous restorative modalities and professionals under one roof. We did our best to design it that way.

MOCWC is a sanctuary for healing. Both Michelle and I want our clients to always feel safe and connected. We chose the oak tree to symbolize MOCWC, since trees characterize being down to earth, grounded and rooted. For me, having lived all over the country, the trees in each place left an imprint on my heart. In Georgia, it was the peach tree. In Florida, the citrus tree. In Missouri, the juniper and maple trees. In Utah, the gorgeous evergreens. In California, it is the eucalyptus and oak trees lining the streets near our building. It is vital that my clients feel rooted in their growth.

Mommy and Lane have relocated, and we are now neighbors. Mommy watches my two bundles of joy a couple of days a week. My doting Dad tells most everyone he meets his daughter is in the mental health business because of him. We all joke that he was my first patient. I am happy to report his business background was an asset to me when I was launching MOCWC. I never billed him for that first session. Maybe I should? Since we opened our doors, his fantastic controller skills—ha, no pun intended—have been a valuable asset.

I love my job, but I am a workaholic. Finding balance between family and work, let alone time to renew with my friends is not easy. Believe me, my obsessive-compulsive tendencies have searched for a foolproof system to not be busy all the time. I find that from week to week, my balancing act constantly changes; it's a difficult maneuver to master.

Often a quick recharge is needed, which may be a date night with my hubby, a book at the beach, or a hair appointment—these grays get aggressive. When I need more R&R, a visit with my siblings in Utah and Colorado, and watching all the cousins run around together makes my spirit shine again. My friends tend to be the ones that suffer most, however. I do my best to contain client hours into a few fourteen-hour days, as well as allocating time for management duties and consultant time with Lane.

The truth is life and parenting are not easy! Both are full of paradoxes and ironies. I always trust my intuition about what needs my attention most in that moment. To hell with the acrobatic act—everything has a way of working itself out. At this point in my life, I am aware of and accept my flaws, and do my best to stay steady, surrounding myself with people who encourage my dreams.

Having the courage to end my first marriage and pursue a career in psychology were the best decisions I ever made. I do believe Lane never took the time to understand psychology before his flippant comment to me when I was in high school. Now there is comfort knowing my father recognizes the importance of the science of psychology and how it brings an abundance of goodness in my life. He attends yoga classes at my center and joins me at every panel and speaking engagement I attend in the community. He is usually my date, as Cameron is working late or watching the kids. Lane, now my biggest advocate, works the room with his oversized smile, introducing himself to everyone as my first patient. My motto remains: "How great it is to be perfectly imperfect."

Georgina

Georgina is not only a "paw-parent," she is also a volunteer at a no-kill animal shelter near her home in upstate New York. Located on several acres of land in the Catskill Mountains, this facility does not receive any government funding, relying heavily instead on tax-deductible contributions from private donors such as Georgina. Dogs have provided this dedicated woman with unconditional love for her seventy years of living, which actually made the shelter a perfect place for our initial conversation.

Georgina never appeared disconcerted or flummoxed, like the high-spirited terrier in an adjacent play area who was flip-spinning in circles. In fact, quite the contrary. The sounds of the animals did not interfere with our interview. As a matter of fact, their activity brought a calm commotion that soothed the sensitive subject matter Georgina was about to reveal. "Feeling repressed for years" was a story she safely ensconced behind her heart's glass house, even though those kinds of houses are notoriously bad places to hide feelings.

Having a bothered conscience is something most women are experts at, but not Georgina. One of her hobbies is collecting vintage handbags. There appears to be no "hindsight guilt" hiding in her closet, with the assortment of designer purses, and shoes, too! She recognizes a certain amount of concealed guilt is good for her, yet she never lets the pain from her past punish her present or paralyze her future.

Currently, Georgina cares for two rescued furry friends, as well as an aging husband. Happily married to her second husband for almost thirty years, she has slowly learned to live into her charmed life. She is confident about the decisions she has made, even though a few are still concealed within a blur.

Nothing empowers someone to heal and grow as much as having self-love and acceptance. This septuagenarian strongly believes that it should be a woman's decision to do what they want with their bodies. One could say that Georgina has never allowed her choices to play with her emotions.

No one says you have to love your parents. I did not love or even like my mother. However, at the end of her life, I was financially responsible for her. My generous husband and I helped buy her a home, and also found her an assisted care facility when she was unable to be alone. I do not feel guilty about the relationship I had with my mom, or how her lack of love affected me throughout my lifetime. Looking back, I appreciated what she did for me growing up. I respected her hard work, while also acknowledging her limitations as a woman with a physical handicap. But gratitude does not equal love.

From my perspective, a parent's responsibilities begin at the birth of their child. I feel it was my mother's responsibility to cultivate a relationship with me when I was young. If she had naturally offered warmth, caring and love, I would have instinctively given those back to her as a child. As a teenager and young adult, it seemed illogical to me that I should create or feel something that was non-existent between us.

Maybe innate common sense was the key to being able to combat my own struggle not to give into regret. When good sense and sound judgment is belabored, I do not experience feelings of shame, and I am not emotionally distressed. I do know my upbringing shielded me from feelings of guilt.

My mother had been confined to bed during her formative years; it was tuberculosis, I believe. As a result, one of her legs was shorter than the other. When they married, my father was twenty years her senior. My mother was thirty-five when I was conceived; my father was fifty-five.

I only know about their relationship from what I have been told, which is not very much. I am completely in the dark about how they met or what any part of their life was like. As I reflect upon and consider the relationship I had with my parents, since I was an only child maybe my mother was jealous of me and the attention my father gave to me and not to her.

I was only thirteen when my father died. My memories of him are unclear. Although I do have a tendency to put him on a pedestal, I remember he was thoughtful, loving and strict.

I vividly recall one picturesque memory sitting next to my father in his leather lounge chair on top of an ugly shag area rug watching boxing together on television.

After he died unexpectedly of a heart attack, my mother provoked me, wanting to know why I would not give her all the love I had given my father. In that moment, and over the course of further heated arguments, she called me a materialistic bitch. I guess these lasting words set the tone for the remainder of our mother/daughter relationship, forcing me to grow up independent, guarded and isolated.

Since I was a latchkey kid, in third grade my parents decided I was old enough to have my first shelter rescue dog. I named her Snickers. A mixed breed, black furry sweetheart, she was my friend and loyal companion until she developed cancer. I was heartbroken. Brown-and-white Jeff-Jeff followed Snickers in my late teens. He needed rescuing from the horrors of being abandoned, and the uncertain life in the local shelter. Somehow I related to his living situation.

I always felt my mother was a study in contradictions. She was very inconsistent in her discipline with me. She would punish me, yet never follow through on the consequence. She would penalize me by not letting me to go to the beach with my friends, but then allow me to skip going to church with her. Then I would either sneak out while she was at church, or catch up on extra sleep.

Much to my mother's displeasure, as a teenager I would go to parties and drink. Yes, I was promiscuous. Yes, I was timid. Yes, I was afraid of getting close to people so I wouldn't be hurt.

As a senior in high school, I received a scholarship to a junior college, which helped pay for some of my tuition and books. My counselor at the time knew someone at the local bank, and they offered me a job. So I worked as a teller and was training to be in the real estate loan department when I realized I was pregnant.

I was never a hundred percent certain who the father was since premarital sex was a good way for me to get attention. I had recently relocated to a strange city while attending college, and the move left me lonely and little depressed. Sex for me was a form of control, and gave me the attention and closeness I lacked from my mother. As I think back to that time, I remember feeling a morsel of panic that I could not love a baby because I really did not know how to love.

After two months of pregnancy, I knew I wanted to have an abortion, since there was *no way* I could support a child. I was still a child myself. My mother was living several hundred miles away, and surely would not have been sympathetic. I tried to find a doctor who would perform an abortion. There were no internet searches possible at that time, and many places were considered to be "back rooms with a coat hanger." I was smart enough to know that with non-medical assistance, having a "back street" abortion was unsafe; it was not the direction I wanted to take. This was prior to the U.S. Supreme Court's Roe v. Wade decision in 1973, when federal law protected a woman's right to choose.

A co-worker told me about a medical doctor who practiced two hours away on a winding mountain road in a remote area in upstate New York. I called his office and scheduled a consultation. The clinic visit was brief. Coming straight to the point he told me, "I do not do abortions. I am sorry that you were misinformed. Unfortunately, I cannot recommend any other physician to help you."

His response was unexpected and a complete shock to me. I wanted to cry, but I didn't. I do not recall spending time thinking about my predicament, just dealing with my next course of action, which was getting home first, then deciding what to do next. I was afraid of driving home at the time because it occurred to me that if my car broke down, or I had an accident on this windy road, no one would ever find me. Although there may have been more feelings involved, I recognized this was the path I had chosen. Now I needed to course correct.

Adoption back in the '60s was hush-hush. Girls "went away" to a convent or a boarding school so that their neighbors never knew about their sexual activities. I recognized I did not feel guilty over the idea of giving my child away, which says a lot about how sure I was that this was the right decision for me. I was not ready to be responsible, nor did I have the resources to be the best possible parent. I was well aware of my inability to care for this child, let alone provide the type of life he or she deserved.

Soon my skirts were getting too snug and I could no longer button them. At five months pregnant, I stopped working. A colleague suggested I see a social worker. That's when I met Irma, who truly was an angel. Not only was she my social worker, she was a mother figure and always made me feel less alone. Irma helped me apply for the welfare program, and lovingly took me into her family. I like to think of her as my substitute mother. I was twenty and here was a caring, fifty-year-old woman who barely knew me but helped me arrange my jumbled life and made me feel loved.

Since I could not afford maternity clothes to fit my changing body, Irma made me a dress to wear. I lived with her daughter Tiffany and took care of Irma's grandbaby. I did what I needed to do and earned my keep. If that meant cleaning the house and changing dirty diapers, I did it. Yet I had to hold my breath since poopy diapers caused me to gag and feel sick to my stomach.

I was alone during the baby's delivery, but relieved and comforted when a female nurse with curly hair held my hand. Another human connection felt nice. The nurse announced, "It is a girl," and I immediately disconnected from the child to whom I had given birth.

The weeks and months flashed by; I went back to living as if nothing had happened. I decided to go back to school to learn bookkeeping, since I wanted something bigger for myself, but didn't know what that would look like. Despite all the tragedy in my life, love never presented itself. I questioned whether if love were to appear, would I even recognize it? Would it come at the expense of every fragment of my being?

After a few years I married a man, yet I wasn't in love with him. It was a slight surprise to me when I was unable to get pregnant. This I believe was for the best. He was a sweet person, but he smothered me. I did not like that. Our relationship felt more like we were brother and sister, which was ultimately what ended it for me in three short years. I had yet to experience that star-crossed sickness of being in love with a man, until two years later when I met my current husband, a very prominent businessman.

Roger was at the height of his career when we met. I was working within his world. We have now been together for a total of forty-seven years. I felt complete warmth and acceptance when I was with him, and a fondness between us like I had never known. We had been together eight years (and not married yet) when we found out I was pregnant, although I had been taking birth control. He had four teenage children from a previous marriage, and he and I were both concerned about how they would react.

Together we were unsure about raising a child, and I was hesitant for many reasons. Did I have the ability to give this child the love and attention he or she required and deserved? This was a looming fear.

I opted to have an abortion.

It would be safe to say much of what happened in my life— the lack of love from my mother, the loss of my father at an early age, and perhaps a deep feeling of abandonment—could have resulted in my numbness. I somehow learned to internalize all my life events. If I were to rationalize and expressively attach emotion to them, I assume my state of mind could have been damaged from my life experiences. I knew this unconsciously, at some level. As I sit here, my heart aches a bit, both physically and emotionally, but the unconditional love I feel comes from my furry friends and my devoted Roger.

Much of my early adult life taught me about the danger of staying in situations that no longer serve me. I feel I was much less fearful in my youth. Being raised in the same tight-knit community, along with attending public school with all my friends made it easy to be outgoing. Growing up, I knew everyone and never felt judged, yet timidity developed for me when I became an adult. I am uncomfortable in new situations, especially with people I do not know.

I do recognize my dogs may have been a substitute for having children or for a deep level of companionship. They too, require care and attention. I believe my canines give back more than they receive in the form of love, laughter and companionship. Bubbles, mostly a white sheltie mix, had a special role in my life for ten years and warmed my heart. Any time I have been without a dog, there was always a yearning for one. My dream is to have a houseful of dogs—well, at least four.

The older and wiser I become, the more I realize there's a lot of grey area in life, more than we are led to believe as children. You can be a good Catholic and take birth control pills. You can be divorced and still believe in marriage. Gigantic ideological gaps exist on both sides for a woman's choice of either abortion or adoption. Ultimately, very few women can really relate until they themselves have either terminated a pregnancy or have given up their baby for adoption.

I have no regrets and I am satisfied with my choices. I am also grateful to have had the ability to choose. With 20-20 hindsight, I see that each decision I made was about being true to myself. Those decisions are still valid to this day. Fifty years ago I wanted to have an abortion, but chose a closed adoption process instead. Only one friend who knew me back then will occasionally ask if I carry any guilt or remorse about my decision. For me, guilt is only created from actual or indirect pressure by someone other than yourself. In other words, doing something you find questionable, or against your own best judgment. I stand firm in my convictions.

If you fast forward five decades, my friend and I continue our conversations, but now we talk about things other than my adoption and abortion experiences. She is the only person who knows my history. Our conversations are varied. She likes to discuss aging-associated diseases and concern for her grown children. My preferred topics include care of my eighty-(plus)-year-old spouse, reviewing current Broadway musicals, and sagas from my daily adventures walking to the dog park, where I relish watching Scooter, my ten-year-old black-and-tan German Shepherd mix, mothering and pro-tecting Susie-Q, my fearful five-year-old jet-black street dog.

What I do know is throughout my life, self-preservation has been my sole responsibility. If *I* did not look after me, who would? Well, maybe my four-legged friends would. They sure do know how to penetrate my armor! I will always find them awaiting my arrival with tails wagging. My darling of a friend just bought me a shirt that says, "All I want to do is hang with my dogs."

Jessie

I had the privilege of getting to know both Jessie* and her twenty-two-year-old son, Inmer Francisco, during my visit to Nicaragua. That country exudes natural warmth and hospitality, despite the sunbaked, barren landscape. Inmer acted as our translator, putting to use his English teaching degree from Universidad Centroamericana. Any language barrier can make an interview a bit challenging, but this young man did a remarkable job for us!

Although enduring many catastrophes in her lifetime, none have broken Jessie's spirit. In fact, the day after her birth on September 30, 1972, a 6.2 magnitude earthquake crumpled and completely destroyed the hospital where she was born. As a mother myself, I was beyond impressed with Jessie's tireless devotion to making her child's dreams come true. In the face of adversity, she displayed how long distance is just a test to see how far love can travel.

---

*Her given name is Thelma Jessenia, but she prefers Jessie.

No matter our circumstances, we have the power to make our life what we want. I am grateful to Jessie for reminding me of this absolute truth and for the permission to share her story. Unfortunately, our conversation was not long enough for me. Yet we parted ways hugging—my favorite form of communication. As Jessie and her son walked away together, I could sense their profound heart-to-heart connection.

On the airplane flying home, I smiled looking at the pictures that were taken of the two of them after our interview. I spotted a similar upturn in their cheeks and enthusiasm in their eyes. While Jessie may have been scared at times, she was present to life and made the best of her circumstances, no matter what else was going on. And unlike the hospital, she never crumbled under the calamities of life.

Running away at seventeen gave me choices. What my future would be, I was uncertain. But I knew in my heart that any-thing would be better than where I was living. I was raised in Tola, a predominantly Catholic community, with my adoptive family. A few thousand people lived in that town when I was growing up; now it has turned into a popular tourist spot.

My birth mother, Dalila, raised me for only a short time. I am sad about that. I remember that she would sometimes smile and sing when she was in a good mood. I was one of three children from three different men. My biological father, Matilde, was an alcoholic and could not support our little family. He drank too much beer, and people would see him passed out on the sidewalk. I never got to know either of my parents very well. I was young, and I do not remember much from that very short time when we lived together.

I was adopted by my father's family when I was seven. My Uncle Roman and Aunt Martha became my adoptive parents. Going to live with another family was difficult for me, but I called them Papa and Mama. Mama was a perfectionist and a little bit fat. Papa had a good heart and always wore hats.

They had eleven natural children. Being the twelfth child, I was treated poorly and blamed for everything. These were not easy times for me. Every couple of days I was punished, yet still to this day, I do not understand why or what I did that was wrong. Maybe it was because I was the only adopted child, and everything was my fault.

Mama would accuse me of playing with my friends and not studying after school. My classmates tried to explain we were all studying together. I liked school, and I liked to learn. I told the truth to Mama and tried to defend myself. But she never believed either me or my friends. It was a very unfair, one-sided situation. The facts never mattered to Mama.

My punishment was being hit with the *coyunda*. With both knees on the ground, I tried not to cry when fifteen lashes would whip my legs on the porch, in front of our neighbors. I cringe every time I think of that cowhide rope. The wounds from those lashings are lifelong.

Growing up, I talked to God. One neighbor, Theresa, was always very friendly to me. She saw everything that took place on our porch. She would invite me over, and I would go to her house. She was the only one who would give me advice, along with making me feel good.

The household I grew up in was full of unfairness. It made me mad, and it was hard for me to keep silent, which caused more whippings. I was tired of being treated like a slave, so I asked God for help. No answers came. Papa gave me love, but it was not enough for me to stay there in that house. I decided to run away when I was seventeen. Mama called the police because she thought I had been kidnapped. I am not sure why she cared where I was. The police never found me.

My friend's sister told me about a job as a housewife in Managua. When I ran away, I went there and was happy to be cooking, cleaning and washing clothes two hours away from Mama and her coyunda. I stayed three years, working for two different families. I enjoyed being in a different city. I met new people, and everyone was nice to me. It was the start of my new life.

I married our neighbor Theresa's son, Francisco, when I was twenty-two. We knew each other growing up, so he was aware of my bad situation at home. He did not like my adoptive parents either. He filled a void in my heart, telling me not to worry because he would always be there for me. His words made my heart go boom-boom! I felt happy!

We had a son together, Inmer Francisco. When my son was three, I separated from my husband because he was a womanizer. Theresa tried to convince me to give him another chance, but each time I did, he would cheat on me again. This happened too many times. Eventually we divorced, and I moved back into Papa's house since Mama was away. It was a much better environment when she was not around.

I wanted to support myself and my son.

Around this time, Inmer developed a fever and started having seizures. He was diagnosed with a form of epilepsy and had to take medicine called Epival to control his attacks. These were scary times for me. Sometimes we could not control him during a seizure, and it required two people to take him to the hospital. These episodes eventually went away with the medication. Yet the medicine and doctor visits were so expensive, I had to go back to Managua to work.

We needed money to pay the bills. I left my son in Tola with his grandmother, Theresa. This provided me comfort. She had always been like a mother to me, which is why I call her Madre. Theresa provided Inmer a stable home and love. I am eternally grateful and continue to thank God daily for putting Theresa in our lives. I knew I had the best woman taking good care of my son. Still, not being with him made my heart sad. For four years I would see Inmer only on Sundays—just four days every month.

When Inmer was seven, I had to move to Costa Rica. There was no work in Nicaragua, and I was desperate. I needed to support my son. I asked many people in Managua for a job, but there was nothing for me to do. So I did not have any other choice but to move.

Looking back, I missed so much of his life when I was in Costa Rica. I experienced so many moments of loneliness not being with my son. Calling and texting was never enough for me. Every December, I would return to Tola, renew my work documents, and see my son for fifteen days each year. Only fifteen days.

Even though I was far away, I loved Inmer unconditionally, and prayed he and I would be back together soon. I wanted my son to have everything that I did not have. Thinking about him kept me motivated to work hard. I had five different jobs as a live-in housewife during my time in Costa Rica. The last family was my favorite; they allowed me to go to church and have more time for God.

My son is very smart; his grades were always good. The university paid all four years of his housing, food, and tuition on scholarship. He graduated in 2015. Despite Mama's accusations, I always liked school and was proud of my good grades. I would have liked to attend university, but the money and opportunity were never there for me. I am happy this was different for Inmer.

My son is now working as a concierge, making his customers happy with his excellent communication skills and nice smile. He works for a local company that caters to tourists and is doing very well. I am so proud of Inmer, and the man he has become. He wants to take care of me now.

At this time, I am reunited with my son after an extremely long fifteen years apart! Being back in my home country is good. I go to church four times a week. Inmer, or as his friends call him, Iain, likes it when I make *espageutis* with beef and plantains for him. Sometimes I make fried snapper. In less than a month, we will be moving into a new house he built for the two of us, with two bedrooms and a large kitchen. It is thirty meters away from Theresa's house in Tola. We are still deciding what color to paint our new *casa*.

Inmer made sure there is enough "kitchen" for me to begin my new occupation. I have started a business making ice cream. My company is called Mana, from the Bible, when mana from heaven came miraculously to the Israelites. I am very happy working at home for myself. No one tells me what to do. It feels great.

I started by making sixty single servings of ice cream a day; now I make one hundred. Each portion is molded into a cup with a wooden stick and can be eaten like a Popsicle. I sell five flavors: coconut, peanut, mixed fruit, strawberry, and Oreo cookie. The Oreo cookie ice cream is the most popular on the street and in the local schools. There are only two ingredients: milk and fruit, no syrups. I buy pure milk, fresh from the cow, at 7:30 every morning.

My life's challenges have made me stronger. I know that now. In my community, I help other girls that have been abused and give them advice. "Conditions can be hard," I tell them, "but never give up." I am enjoying having more time for myself, and I'm hoping to go to Argentina soon to see my boyfriend. We met when we both were working in Costa Rica. He recently visited me in Nicaragua and met my son. Iain thinks that I am "totally in love with him."

I have no regrets. My past is the past. I only focus on the future. I have missed much of my son's life, yet I look forward to enjoying our new experiences together. I cannot change or take back his childhood, or mine, but now we get to make up for the time that we lost.

Petra

When I was in London, I visited Camden Market's West Yard where Petra, founder of KERB, has organized thirty-four food stalls as a permanent part of the market along the Regent's Canal. KERB is a street food organization of eighty-plus mobile and permanent traders (aka food trucks) that are transforming street food in London one poke bowl at a time. KERB's objective is to place these mobile kitchens in redevelopment areas, bringing life and soul back to the streets.

As I made my way toward the congested scene, I noted fervor from the crowd, along with a fusion of smells wafting through the air. It was a lively setting as people of all ages and ethnicities were indulging in a variety of eatables from vegan curry pies, to chicken, cabbage and corn dumplings. KERB can also be found operating in an exciting, innovative way in five other culinary hubs across London.

A few months later, Petra and I met up in New Orleans where she is taking a bit of time off in a town where fruitiness and flavor go hand in hand. This extraordinary woman is looking to be inspired by that unique city, famous for its cuisine, music and celebrations, as she shapes the next adventure in her story.

Dubbed the "Queen of Street Food," it seemed only natural that our time together started over a long lovely dinner. Conversation flowed like both the bubbly and the vino we were sipping, along with an assortment of dishes ranging from crispy chicken livers to sweet cornbread and wild boar sausage. For Petra, a chocolate connoisseur, the meal was not complete without the super-chocolaty crémeux, a spin on a classic pudding.

She rode her bike over to meet me at my hotel the following morning. We chatted over coffee for me, and Emergen-C vitamin drink mix for Petra. Her daily wellness routine and health habits are indeed impressive. Over our two days together, we realized that neither of us is keen on small talk, yet acknowledged that polite conversation is a crucial social lubricant. She and I took the most pleasure in talking about the things that really matter to us, in addition to what we are willing to do to make our dreams become reality.

I was brought up in Brent Eleigh, a village of one hundred people located in Suffolk County, England. One of my most vivid memories from my early years was walking around the garden with my Mum, Miranda, whom I adore—just the two of us. I was four-years-old and had not started school yet. At one point, I recall walking past the boxed hedges and noticing the lavender, rosemary and sweet peas swaying in the breeze. I turned to her and asked, "Do we live forever?"

"No, we don't," she told me. "We go to heaven when we die."

I have never forgotten the feeling of devastation I had at that moment, becoming aware for the first time that life has limits.

Our family lived in the converted stables on an incredible playground of land located within the grounds of my paternal grandparents' home. It was coined the "Peppermint Palace" by the Americans who'd fly over it in WWII. It boasted a lake, a swimming pool, a croquet lawn and a huge area of sprawling woods. Growing up, I wanted to live in town with all the other kids. But as I look back at my childhood now, it was a magical place to roam and run—so full of adventure!

My Dad, Tristram, was an herb grower. He loved being in his garden shed, potting herbs and watching them grow. I remember some of my packed school lunches, often complete with earwigs, featuring Dad's "rustic fayre" from the garden. Connected to the land, a very visceral guy, he taught farming in Zaire, in central Africa during the first year of my life. My Mum, older brother and I went with him. I believe that the time I spent deep in the Congo has influenced me in ways I will never truly understand.

My parents were not linear; they lived in the moment. I had a certain amount of structure and boundaries in my life growing up, but it was pretty free and easy—generally center-ing in the here and now. There wasn't a lot of money; in fact, you could say we were broke much of the time, but the friends and the fun and the adventures always flowed freely.

My father bought a pig farm on a mountain in Tuscany in the '70s. As you can imagine, the impact that going to Tuscany every summer had on our whole family was huge. To this day, *Monte Amiata* represents a very poignant place for us. Our world revolved around food; it was the main subject discussed in our family. To this day, I believe good food should be enjoyed and eaten by everybody, just like it is in Italy, which is where I spent such a large portion of my childhood.

I was a shy, yet curious child. Over the years, I attended numerous schools and needed to continuously adapt. Luckily, school was easy for me. I was a good student and making friends was never a problem. Both my brothers are dyslexic though, and went to boarding school for extra academic help. Dyslexia runs throughout the branches of our family tree, which makes for some interesting spelling in Christmas cards!

My father's laughing brown eyes closed upon the light of this world when I was sixteen, which is exactly when mine were truly beginning to open. My father's fatal car accident was the biggest shock of my life, and the worst thing that had happened to our family. Although the grief was intense, the support after his death was overwhelming. Many, many people showed up for us. That was lovely.

Experiencing my dad's death at such a young age made me acutely aware that life should be about following your dreams. I am intensely a "feelings" person. I live my life based on what I feel, although being driven by emotions can be challenging!

One of the things I recognized about my incredible loss is that it enabled me to come out of my dad's shadow and no longer defer to him. His absence forced me to become a bigger character. It may have happened anyway, yet his death definitely sped up the maturation process for me.

At that time, so I could be closer to home, I transferred back to a local school. Just sixteen, my social life was kicking in. I was going out with my friends and dancing all night; the rave culture was a big thing in England then and it was enrapturing.

For a time, I tried sticking to the conventional script. At twenty-three, with a degree in American studies from Manchester, I spent a year trying to follow the traditional path to land a good job in London. I got my wish quite quickly, working as an assistant casting director for TV commercials and pop promos. It was a lot of fun, yet I longed to get out on the open seas. A year later, unable to stay in one place any longer, I booked a one-way ticket to Antibes in the South of France, and began searching for my first job on a private super-yacht.

A chance encounter involving a friend picking up a hitch-hiker who turned out to be a captain of a 53-meter yacht led to my first break. ("Are you looking for a stewardess by any chance? If so, I have just the person for you.") The answer was "Yes!" I had finally landed my first big paying job! While on this boat, I learned tolerance, along with the art of serving people without being servile. However, the sense of boredom and glib comfort as I watched the super-rich was saddening to me. Meanwhile, below deck we were having a wild old time of it. Living such an extreme existence was amazing to me. I experienced countless highs and feelings of entrapment, along with a mild madness at life. Floating in a huge capsule with the same people that I had to find a way of getting on with, whatever the weather. It was truly a formative time for me, some of the hardest work I've ever done, and crazy, crazy fun.

My takeaway from those four years as a stewardess on luxury yachts was that the world could be my playground. I realized that travel is like oxygen for me. I don't know how else to explain it. Aside from cementing my globetrotting ways, I learned not be contained or corrupted by that. I realized too, that I had outgrown life at sea, and in 2004 I left.

Back home in London in January of the following year, and now pursuing a career in food service, the idea for "Choc Star" hit me like a bolt of lightning. I decided I would buy a truck, turn it into a choc-mobile and drive around selling brownie fudge sundaes, triple chocolate milkshakes, ice creams, truffles and real hot chocolate to anybody and everybody. Chocolate has always been a source of nourishment to me on all levels. From whipping up chocolate layer cakes as a child, to eating homemade chocolate chip cookie dough out of the fridge as a student at Manchester, it was always about the chocolate.

I was first aware of street food when I was ten-years-old in Mexico in 1986. Mum and Dad took our family around that country on chicken buses for a month. What an eye-opener— the sights, the sounds, the smells! I have never forgotten that first whiff from the streets, the taste of maize in the tortillas, or the sound of them being pat, pat, patted in the markets. We all loved the excitement and unpredictable nature of travel, despite the doses of culture shock that came from always straying off the beaten path. That's when the travel bug first took hold of me.

I believe there is beauty in "jumping" without knowing where you are going to "land." It was an incredible feeling to take a risk and buy, unseen, a white Leyland DAF van off eBay. I remember my whole body quivering with delight as my friend and I drove that trusty old ice cream van from Scotland down to London in four days. As scary as it is to jump, I realized I was more scared of not jumping and not following my gut instincts. I liken the feeling to an almost desperate state. The unknown was more familiar to me than the expected.

Choc Star was a combination of wanting to continue traveling, to see more of Britain after so much time in other countries, and to curate a great chocolate experience for people. The reality of actually starting the business and making that dream a reality was terrifying. I had to be the boss, cook, driver, accountant and sales force all at once, often in the rain! There were times when it was hell and totally grueling. I was often on my knees, so to speak, but I kept going, largely because of the incredible human connection I got every time I opened up the hatch and served chocolate lovers like me on the streets.

Ultimately, if the voice in your head says your idea is not sensible, and if that voice is stronger than your gut feeling, than that mental opinion will most likely win. Thankfully, my deep-seated feeling in those key moments has always been stronger. That's my compass. I may operate as a "feeler," yet I approach situations pragmatically with a "builder" mentality.

The more I traded—at markets, festivals, weddings, fetes—the more I bonded with the great, natural community of fellow traders pitching up next to me. After a while I began to consider with them the question I had been pondering— why not organize ourselves into something more? Could we create more visibility, more opportunities, more innovation, more strength in numbers and even better food if we combined forces? Little did I know where that sudden moment of clarity would lead.

KERB was an idea that started as a hobby called "eat.st," which then gathered momentum through organizing other street food traders, and ultimately turned into a bona fide business in October 2012. We are recognized as a street food movement that puts on street food markets and events across the city. KERB acts as a connector, bringing a multitude of flavors, cultures and backgrounds in one place for customers to experience. We have a binding communal component, as food is a universal language. We also believe that through exploring new cuisines, the act of eating can create cultural bonds, even if only for a moment.

KERB grew out of a combination of things. One was England's "bland and boring" food reputation. When I would visit America people would say, "Oh poor you, living in England—the food is so bad there!" Then I would get really angry! This was a big motivator for me when I set up KERB, to build something that the rest of the world could look at and exclaim, "Wow! What an exciting food scene that country has created!"

Being a "foodie" in Britain used to be an elitist thing. I remember people obsessing over the salami they brought back from Italy, or name-checking their olive oils with friends. It was a status thing to be a foodie, and it never really sat right with me.

KERB is about democratizing good food. A renaissance is taking place in Britain's van-based cuisine, found not just in streets and markets, but also at festivals, parties, conventions and just about any other event. And we are disrupting the corporate catering scene by connecting authentic traders from the street with big private events.

I credit my parents with instilling in me the idea that "people are people." In other words, the sense that there is no difference between anyone—the prince or the pauper. Mum and Dad were not snobs in any way; they welcomed all walks of life to our table. The common denominator among all my parents' friends was good energy, good company and gracious spirit. This exposure taught me not to be intimidated by appearance or social codes, which is something I have tried to incorporate into KERB. Our company manual states, "We are people-centric, treating the janitor and the CEO just the same."

KERB grew into a conscious movement, enhanced by my continued education, culminating in a master's degree in urban studies from University College London. Ultimately, like many people, I am driven by the sense of wanting to make a difference and to disrupt the conventional narrative.

I was born ambitious, and part of me always wanted to do something big. As a child, I assumed it would be in an office in a skyscraper, Working Girl-style, making a lot of money. As I have gotten older, I now understand it is more about creating change in the world.

Cities need street food. A healthy city is a place where everyone comes together, shoulder-to-shoulder, treating each other as equals. Humanity needs to stop dividing itself. We're not that different after all. Nothing brings people together like food. At KERB, we love to animate urban spaces. So much of our behavior as we move through cities is so choreographed now:

This is where you walk.

This is where you shop.

This is how you behave.

I love the way markets and street food mess that up, enabling everyone to negotiate among each other for space, sharing stories, connecting with other cultures through food, and making direct transactions with the person cooking your lunch. So simple, yet so important.

This dynamic, often political, and definitely rambunctious business was born out of my love of food and my love of people. It is a distillation, I suppose, of my childhood. Putting good food cooked by passionate entrepreneurs out on the street, making a bit of noise, and creating enticing smells—my father would appreciate the spontaneity. He'd also appreciate the ruffling of feathers in a well-ordered urban space.

The potential with KERB is limitless, and it will always be part of what I do and who I am. I am fortunate to have Simon, a wonderful comrade, at the helm now, while I am on the sidelines. He is obsessed with its success and has the energy and business-head needed to drive it forward. If street food had been trendy before I started Choc Star and KERB, I probably would have never gotten into it in the first place. I guess I am more drawn to doing something that has never been done before.

I wish I was the kind of person to be happy just rolling along, surrounded by everything and everyone I know. Being comfortable is lovely, but when being comfortable becomes uncomfortable, that's a problem for me. I think there is something amazing about putting yourself in a challenging situation where you have to survive on your wits. That's what makes me feel really alive.

The more often I jump, the more confident I become in doing it. Taking this most recent leap of faith—coming to the United States on sabbatical—has uprooted my life once again. There's something here for me that I must explore, yet I can't quite put my finger on what it is or what's next. In extreme moments, I feel simultaneously exhilarated and terrified. Then I remember this is part of the process and that switching lanes isn't supposed to be seamless. It's that feeling of vitality that allows me to recreate myself and forge new paths. I can't wait!

Ruth

Certain people come into your life at just the right moment. Like a modern day village elder, Ruth provided the precise input I needed to produce the proper output at that specific moment in time. That was over fifteen years ago. Indeed, her insight, guidance and unforgettable coffee (infused with cardamom pods and cinnamon sticks) left a permanent imprint on me.

Not long ago, I reflected back and realized with a shock that it had been ten years since we last saw each other, so I contacted her to set up a date. Ruth met me at the Boston Logan International Airport in her car named Nellie, after Roy Roger's Jeep, Nelly Belle. The driverless technology paid little attention when Ruth teased "Whoa, Nellie." I chuckled. Through a wicked lightening show, the three of us ventured north along the rugged Maine coastline.

In retrospect, no matter how long it had been since Ruth and I last talked, we could always pick up right where we left off. The Cliff House in Ogunquit was a spectacular setting, with wide windows displaying striking Atlantic Ocean views. Over coffee, Ruth and I toasted the lobstermen who were out in force that morning. My dear friend never ceases to amaze me with her razor-sharp wit and intellect. Amazingly, she stays relevant and up-to-date on the latest technology—even at seventy-three. It was her innate inquisitiveness that established her as an early proponent of new technologies and gadgets.

We ended our visit near the Nubble Lighthouse with a hug and a piece of Maine's famous blueberry pie. I wished we could have lingered together longer. Ruth is a trailblazing woman who was at the forefront of telecommunications, but she does not think she is "cool" or "interesting." To me she is both. I admire her huge heart, along with her insatiable curiosity.

My granddaughter Amy laughs at my computerized devices. "Grannies aren't supposed to know that stuff!" she tells everybody. I'm the go-to person for electronic gadgets in my family, so "Gadget Gramma" became my moniker, even on Twitter.

I've always done weird things in a peculiar way. My parents supported my strangeness from the time I was very young. My mother expected me to do girly things, but my father encouraged me to be me. So I climbed trees and crashed bikes just like the boys. I remember when I was four I repeatedly rearranged the chairs in the kitchen to create "rooms."

The back of each chair was a part of the labyrinth. Then I would walk through the maze again and again, changing it every time. Creating and defining spaces was something I enjoyed both then and now. My 3D perspective began at an early age for me, I'm sure.

I started dating Bob in 1960 when I was sixteen. We were in the same high school class. After graduating from Lasell College at twenty with an associate's degree in 1964, I stepped into the workforce, marrying Bob in 1965. I quit work a year later and gave birth to Dave when I was twenty-one, Carolyn at twenty-three and Michelle at twenty-five. I went back to work at twenty-nine, not by choice, but to protect the hand-built log house Bob and I had constructed together. We needed a second income. I secured a secretarial position at the Norton Company, a large manufacturing outlet specializing in sandpaper, grinders and ceramic products. It wasn't a very special job, but it helped keep our home out of foreclosure.

Norton offered educational support for their employees, which I decided to take advantage of. In 1978, I graduated with a BA degree in business administration from Clark University. I was drawn to computer programming and intrigued by Fortran, an early programming language. During my studies, I recall writing a program that was a complete dud. It took me a week to find the bug; when I did, I realized I had typed just one lowercase "l" instead of a numeral "1."

Over the years, Bob and I began to grow apart. I was a wife and mother, but I also had a full-time job and attended night school three times a week. It wasn't easy. Dave, Carolyn and

Michelle at the time were in elementary school when I had my heaviest workload. Bob worked construction, so he was home early and took care of the children when I was gone. This was instrumental in helping me manage everything. Ultimately, Bob and I separated in 1980, when I was thirty-six. By that time, the kids were self-sufficient. Dave and Carolyn were in high school and Michelle was in junior high when I designed and built a passive solar house in Charlton and moved the children into this new home. Bob and I did not actually divorce until he wanted to remarry three years later, yet we always maintained an amicable relationship for the children.

It was a challenge juggling family and work. I recall a time when I couldn't even afford to buy nylons. As a single mom, somehow I made it work. My only goal was just to stay afloat. I was focused on helping my offspring get through school, in addition to working on completing the house that I had designed. It really does take a long time to finish everything when you do it yourself.

After getting my degree in 1978, I had moved into a management position at Norton, which is where I met my future husband, Ajay. We were drawn to each other by our fascination with technology. I also think he liked my ponytail. We started off on rocky ground, however. I got annoyed with his eagerness to "help" me. While learning Fortran at the university, I worked on my assignments on Norton's computers. One day, Ajay looked at my task, and he promptly sat down and completed the entire project. I was angry because he had taken all the fun out of it by doing it for me!

The male-dominated environment at Norton could have been a challenge if I had made it so, but overall, it worked out very well. I could relate to men, possibly from my tree climbing and bike crashing days. In the early '80s at Norton, I was hooking my computer keyboard to a telephone receiver's "acoustic coupler." No monitor. No mouse. No hard disk. The coupler served as a modem, transmitting my keyboard signals over the telephone line to a remote computer. This was the cutting edge of technology before the birth of the internet as we know it. In time, I became a systems analyst and was involved with programming systems using the first generation of IBM personal computers.

How awesome is that? We've clearly come a L-O-N-G way in a very short time.

The next generation of computers came with black and white monitors, without a mouse, and without an internal hard disk drive. Instead, there was a slot for a floppy disk. My first PC with a hard disk, in the mid-1980s, came with a five MB drive. Today, that amount of memory wouldn't even power a smartphone.

Right after I moved into the two-story passive solar home I had built in Charlton, I began to have a bit of trouble with the new manager, so I left Norton. I temporarily took a job selling solar panels to heat domestic hot water, but I quickly realized sales was not my strong suit. Subsequently, I was hired at Component Manufacturing Systems (CMS) to create a new IT department, installing computer systems, training employees, and writing documentation to convert the company's manufacturing process from paper to computer. They manufactured the cables and connectors for all the new computers and digital gadgetry, but it was seventy miles away from where we lived.

CMS was a fascinating experience, although it was a grueling job requiring long hours, on top of the ninety-minute drive to and from work. I remember spending one day encouraging a timid sixty-year-old woman who was still recovering from the shock of losing the fight for her dearly loved *manual* typewriter when it was replaced with an *electric* typewriter. Then she had to substitute a computer keyboard for her electric typewriter. She resisted me as much as possible; then she amazed me by becoming quite comfortable with the keyboard.

A high-powered career was never in my sightline. I had actually turned down a couple of opportunities for advancement because I was overwhelmed with the medical/mental challenges that affected my youngest daughter Michelle, who was diagnosed with bipolar and schizoaffective disorder. I just didn't want any more responsibilities at work. I was always a mother first; someone who values close personal relationships second; and third, a "wacky" working woman.

I worked at CMS for two years before moving on to Digital Equipment Corporation (DEC) in 1984. Ajay, whom I had worked with at Norton, was already part of that team. Our relationship had already turned serious. We built our house in Harvard together in 1988 and married in 1989. My son Dave was away in flight school, Carolyn was in college, and Michelle lived with Ajay and me.

On the flip side, when Ajay became involved in my house-building projects, he would get upset with me because I wouldn't listen to his suggestions. Although our basic values are complementary, most of our habits, preferences and interests are opposing. To this day we get on together. Our cultural and personality differences were a challenge at first, but now we can laugh at and delight in our incongruities.

I landed in the marketing department at DEC and held several jobs from technical support to demo development and product management. These were the best years of my career. I traveled extensively, most memorably to Japan and Australia. Our team attended computer shows and demonstrated technology years ahead of its time and before anyone was ready. It was great fun being involved with the birth of the internet, email, online chatting, and then the World Wide Web. You could feel the competition in the air. Now we had color monitors, Microsoft Windows, and a mouse.

Back then we techie people led the way on this new technological adventure. We were split into three groups: developers, users and non-users. The developers were on the cutting edge at the engineering level, creating hardware and software. The users learned how to use the hardware and software for business purposes, usually in large corporations where it was seen as a productivity improvement. The non-users were the vast majority at that time and were unaware of the technology being developed and its future impact on them. Now we are still in the same three groups, but the majority of people fall into the "user" group.

In the late 1980s, we DEC-ish folk demonstrated new technology for the first video conferencing software. We thought it was wicked awesome, yet we were so far ahead of the times that our audience couldn't appreciate its potential. Why would people go to all that trouble to set up such a system when they could just poke their head in the door to chat or pick up a phone?

When introducing new products to the general public, I attempted to create my demos to be as visual as possible. Engineers are clever and technical, but rarely see their product through the untrained user's eyes, often creating something only they know how to use. My job was to bridge the gap and support these gifted engineers, helping them to add or modify features that a typical user could understand. It was important to me that the users understood what I was presenting. If they didn't, I asked them to be honest and upfront; then I would try to offer them a different explanation.

Before the '90s, if a change was made to one document, someone had to manually alter the data in all related documents. At a symposium in Japan in 1992, I demonstrated a new technology that we now refer to as "links." I created a document and linked it to another document so that both could be updated when one was changed, and the user could also access either document with the link. We take that for granted now, but at first it was an exciting, awe-inspiring technology.

My advice to anyone today is to hang on to your hat; technology will continually change by leaps and bounds. Even people working in specific areas cannot know everything that is happening in other related fields and certainly not in unrelated fields. Everything will change: the way we interact with apps and data, the way programs are created, and the way coding keeps morphing to include more and more functionality. Truly, the User Interface is the key to success or failure. No matter how much the hardware or software can do, if a user has no idea how to make use of it, it's useless.

I left DEC after nine enjoyable years and phased into quasi-retirement. Even now, I continue to take classes on networking, computer security and computer aided 3D design for architectural purposes. Currently, I am learning Swift, created by Apple to build apps for Apple devices via an online class. I plan to use it to develop my own app, a list management system for tasks that need to be completed and organized in order of priority. I still have plenty "to do" on my list.

I continue to hone my gadgetry skills and become extremely excited anytime I have the opportunity to design/build/renovate another home using 3D computer software. It brought me great joy to buy and overhaul a home close to my son and granddaughter a few years back. I refurbished the entire house, while also creating two networks: one for all the home automation gadgetry, and one for computers and mobile devices.

I had planned to retire my tools at seventy, but now at seventy-three, I can't imagine it. I don't want to slow down, but I eventually will someday, I guess. With no official retirement in sight for Gadget Gramma, I'm still at the "cutting edge" for the old geezers group. We just purchased another piece of land to build our retirement home in Massachusetts, as Ajay plans to retire within a few months.

This next house I'm designing with 3D CAD software will incorporate all of our favorite features from all of our other houses, plus a few extras. It will also be designed as a "Universal House" design, aka "Age in Place" to accommodate any physical condition we may find ourselves in during the last few decades of our lives. Since creating plans for houses inspires me so much, I plan to complete this project, and then hopefully start future adventures after getting settled into our new place.

As we age, Ajay and I enjoy laughing about the past, reflecting on the specialized high-tech changes that have become commonplace in just the past thirty years. The next generation of technology will change everything again, twice as fast, right before our elderly eyes.

My birthday is coming, but seventy-four is the new thirty-four in my mainframe mind.

Khorshed

*More than a simple risk taker, Khorshed Wadia Ezekiel, known
as Khatu to her close family and friends, had a feisty spirit and
a generous soul. She never met a person in need that she didn't
help. For many people young and old, Khorshed was a guiding
light, treating everyone equally with kindness and compassion
without any trace of judgment or prejudice.*

*Her clever commentary on a vast range of subjects not
only impressed her family, but also everyone who met her. She
mastered the ability to incorporate cooking, art, culture and
poetry into her daily bag of tricks. Those who knew Khatu were
captivated with her multifaceted personality and impressed with
her self-determination. She proved throughout her life that there
is a difference between having multiple talents and being interested
in diverse activities.*

*My friend and Khatu's younger brother, Dr. Maneck
Wadia, connected me with his nephew, Gul Fraaz (Gulu) when*

I was in New Delhi, India two years ago. I instantly liked this chivalrous man. Taking time out of his busy schedule to pick me up at my hotel, Gulu and I had dinner at a popular Parsi restaurant, Soda Bottle Opener Walla *in the Khan Market. This family favorite happens to also be near the Parsi graveyard where Khatu has been laid to rest.*

As the hostess led us up the creaky wooden stairs to our table, Gulu pointed out the framed black and white photograph of his maternal grandparents hanging on the wall. I quickly realized that it must be an honor to have your photo mounted on the wall of a restaurant you didn't own. I now had a deeper insight into this family's prominence within their community.

During our gastronomic journey, Gulu offered me a glimpse into the family heritage and the unique religious choices Khatu made for herself and her future family. Even after her death, she has been labeled a rational rebel by many who knew her, and I was just beginning to understand the reason for this.

After my visit to India, additional queries about this incredible woman led me to Gulu's brother, Jawahar, who lives in Portland, Oregon. Both sons extoled the teachings of their mother, and were obviously impacted by her kind-heartedness and generosity. My story of Khatu emanates mostly from her two doting sons.

At the time of my initial visit to New Delhi, Khatu was living with Gulu, but was unable to participate in an interview due to her deteriorating health. What I learned from her son is that for eighty-nine years, beginning when she was in college, Khatu made a visible and vibrant impact on the theatrical stage.

Throughout her life she exuded a profoundly confident stage presence that became her signature style.

I am sorry to say, I never met this dynamic diva with her multitude of talents, to which this piece cannot begin to do justice. She passed away four months before I contacted Gulu to request permission to include her in this book. I felt strongly that her story needed to be told in the first person like the rest of these remarkable women. Please note that a considerable amount of this chapter was taken from previously published articles in the Parsiana Magazine, *in addition to a fifty-page memorial tribute book,* A Life Worth Living *written by Gulu.*

Khorshed Wadia Ezekiel, like all of us, was given the gift of time on this earth to live, learn, love and also leave a legacy. This particular written portrait is a tribute to a woman who made a profound impression on many people by simply staying true to herself.

Throughout my life, I have played many different roles. Aside from being a daughter, sister, wife, mother, colleague, collaborator and friend, I am a Parsi.

We Parsis have descended from the Persian Zoroastrians who have integrated themselves into India's society, yet we keep our own distinct customs and traditions. In fact, the Zoroastrians in India have two communities: the Parsis who came first to India between the 8th and 10th century to escape religious persecution in Persia (now Iran), and the Iranis who followed centuries later.

My autonomous streak, as well as my need for personal enrichment, precluded me from settling into an arranged marriage as most other young women did at that time. My parents pressured me with suitors in our Parsi community who did not understand nor accept my independence, varied interests and passions. I turned them all down.

I gave up the life of luxury and ease of my childhood when I walked out on my wealthy parents to marry a tall, dark, dashing naval officer of Bene-Israeli Jewish descent. The Parsi Zoroastrian community I lived in would never traditionally accept a woman who marries outside the faith. Any woman who made that choice would be shunned and ex-communicated immediately.

In India, marriages have always been regarded as alliances between families for the purposes of reproduction and economic stability. Today, the role of women in the Indian society is changing, as it slowly is throughout the world as well.

I was twenty-eight when I married the love of my life, Joe Ezekiel. Yet this was considered a late marriage for an Indian woman. Joe and I were kindred spirits, sharing a love of art, culture, history and theater. However, my defiant actions caused chaos within my family circle; my strict Parsi parents promptly disowned me. I left home without a *paisa*, which is to a *rupee* what a cent is to a dollar. I soldiered on, settling into a middle class and happy life living in Bombay (now Mumbai) in the mid-1950s.

I know that throughout my lifetime my dogged determination caused a great deal of turmoil for my traditional

Parsi parents. Yet, this never stopped me from firing back with patriotic zeal. I regularly participated in processions demanding liberation from the British. During one of the marches in the streets of Bombay, I even stomped on the foot of one of the policemen, who howled in pain. I became very active in the movement for independence; in 1948, at the first post-Independence Congress session held in Jaipur, I earned the honor of sitting at the podium near Prime Minister Jawaharlal Nehru. What a moment! I was so proud of us all.

Innate social justice was at the core of my being. My values rest on the foundation of respect and honor for everyone's individual choices, along with equal treatment for all, without discrimination. During my college days in the '40s, I was also an early supporter of gay rights in India. When a close friend of mine and fellow theater doyen took his life in his early twenties, partly due to the stigma attached to being gay at that time, it shattered my world.

As in many other cultures, religion can play a prominent role in the decisions a person makes. It was evident in my life that there was a constant battle between the liberal and the orthodox. I knew my choices were right at the time, yet I cannot deny that it was difficult being alienated from my loved ones, my culture, and my religion. Most of my siblings continued to speak with me, but one in particular felt I had betrayed the family and turned his back on me for many years. However, with time and the birth of my three children, Raina, Jawahar and Gulu, this familial nonsense eventually resolved and everyone accepted my children, husband and I. After all, no matter what the culture or religion, grandparents cannot resist grandkids.

When I made the choice to give up a life of ease to marry the man I love, the course of my life changed—for the better. Staying true to myself and my culture, I would proudly wear my *sari*, our traditional dress, along with my red *bindi*, the decorative circle worn by married women in the middle of their foreheads that signifies true love and prosperity. In fact, one time I painted a *bindi* on my forehead with indelible bright red nail polish to eliminate the tedious task of putting on a new one every day.

My husband's career path kept us constantly on the move. When we married, Joe was posted with the Indian Navy in Bombay, our hometown. After the birth of our youngest, Gulu, in 1959, he joined Hindustan Steel Ltd., located first in Durgapur, West Bengal, and then became head of the Dusseldorf and London offices where we lived from 1964-67. On our return to India we moved back to Durgapur where he held a senior position.

Joe then took a post as a Professor of Business and Materials Management at the Indian Institute of Management in Calcutta (now Kolkata). Once he retired from his ambitious career, we moved yet again to Madras (now Chennai), where he took up freelance management assignments, traveling extensively to the Far East and Brazil.

Since we moved more than the average family, our three kids became very adaptable. Being half Parsi and half Jewish, people often asked, "What's that combination called?" Our cultural blending became a topic of conversation wherever we went. My husband's parents were pioneers in the reform movement in India, and very liberal and open minded. Traditionally in Judaism, children most often take the religion of the mother. In Zoroastrianism (the religion of the Parsis), it's the father's religion. However, by Indian law, the children assume the same religion as their father.

So where does that leave my kids? Only God knows.

Since Joe and I wanted to stay eclectic, we celebrated festivals of all religions—but oddly never Jewish or Parsi traditions at home. My intentions were unpretentious; since both of us were non-practicing in our family's religion, we were determined not to influence our kids towards the respective religions we grew up with in any way.

As a family, we would regularly go caroling with our Christian friends, attend Holi and Diwali, traditional Hindu festivals with our Hindu neighbors, and enjoy biryani, a rice dish, with our wonderful Muslim friends. It was important for us that our offspring were culturally intelligent. We wanted them to understand their ancient cultural heritage, as well as the history of the Bene-Israeli Jewish and Parsi Zoroastrian communities. But ultimately, as they got older, our "half-n-half" kids called themselves "Par-Brews," which to me sounded like a sweet, exotic coffee.

The bottom line is that, leaving out the religious aspect, I am proud all three of my children have both Jewish and Parsi blood. In my heart, I believe the greatest gift that we as parents have given our children is the ability to proudly claim and be part of two great religions and cultural communities, each full of history and a rich way of life. Rather than limiting their outlook, it has broadened their minds and opened their eyes.

Filling our home with music, good food and laughter was another integral part of our family life. After starting a career as a chef in his early twenties, my elder son, Jawahar sometimes showed off his newfound cooking skills. *Reader's Digest* published what I had penned about him making Spaghetti Bolognese at home. It went something along the lines of, "My son is a wondrous cook. With one glance, you can tell his food will taste Heavenly, even though my kitchen looks like Hell."

Humor has always been the best prescriptive medicine for me. It has been especially therapeutic during the last three-and-a-half years while I was gravely ill. My son, Gulu staged impromptu one-man skits when I was bedridden during the lowest points of my life. He'd recite nonsensical rhymes about three things I love: cats, chocolate and children. Gulu would tell me, "Mum you look cute today." And I would reply, "Not cute, but *acute!*"

We often host guests at our house, and to the dismay of some of them, I have been known to suddenly begin a whole new conversation just as they were at the door getting ready to leave. These extended goodbyes often made my kids impatient, since my gift of gab could easily add another half-hour to the guests' visit. When they complain, I remind them to drain and squeeze as much joy as possible from every minute of life, because that minute will never come back.

Author's note: Khorshed passed away on October 19, 2016. This chapter was written with help from Gulu and Jawahar Ezekiel, as well as Dr. Maneck and his wife, Harriet Wadia. I wish to extend my heartfelt thanks to all of them for answering my endless questions in order to chronicle memories of Khatu accurately. Most important, each of them offered profound insight into her steadfast examples of what unconditional love and self-determination look like in real life. I am hopeful that someday I will meet this highly complex woman when I cross over to the other side.

Sonia Marie

While being a selfless mother and wife, Sonia Marie maintains her individuality, which is not an easy undertaking. Neither is doing your best to stay present despite serious health matters concerning yourself and your family.

I met Sonia Marie for the first time at the Curious Fork, a one-stop shop offering cooking classes, culinary supplies, and a counter-serve café. She was accompanied by Jacob, her charming eighteen-year-old son. He appeared rather mature for his age, offering a heartfelt hug as a salutation. Although our visit was brief, we quickly exchanged pleasantries, since she and Jacob had prior commitments. Sonia Marie mentioned their recent family trip to Croatia, through Sensory Adventures, where she accompanied a group of clients as the nutritionist, assuring that the food on their trip was healthy and nutritious for everyone.

A month later we met again, this time just the two of us, at a hotel located in the quaint beachside community that holds a special place in her heart. Sonia Marie sipped lemon water, while proudly reminiscing about the many summers spent in this place when her boys were younger. At that time, she was still married and living in Los Angeles. Both Josh and Jacob would count the days before they could go to the beach, attend summer camps, and spend time with their cousins for two months seaside. All of these memories lit up her striking hazel eyes. Family clearly matters to her.

As a Holistic Nutrition Coach, she strives to impact and educate everyone she meets about how to keep fit and in good health using her own personal experiences as evidence. Sonia Marie influences her clients' behavior by helping them shape life goals, while offering a sense of direction and an inspiration to live a healthy life. A deep gladness radiates from her when she talks about her life decisions and the motivation that always seemed to be connected to her vocation. With courage and composure, Sonia Marie has progressed through difficult stages, staying rooted in her purpose and responsibilities to herself, her family, and her clients.

She preaches that doing the same thing each and every day, by eating the same food or exercising the same way will always get you the same results. So she encourages everyone to think more creatively. Sonia Marie is forever writing in her journals about alternative ways to break through challenges and negative habit patterns, and to organically innovate and construct new pathways to healthy sustainable living, both physically and intellectually.

Her story reminds me sometimes that as women, we have to go through our worst to arrive at our best. Sonia Marie acquired wisdom through living, not in the absence of problems, but in her remarkable ability to deal with them. Even when times are tough, this gracious woman is a prime example that no pain comes without a purpose.

I grew up in Cajun country, so of course, food was a huge part of my life. My grandmother lived right behind our home in Lafayette, Louisiana. I would sit on her countertop and watch her effortlessly pull off dinner for our large family like no one's business! One day I asked if I could help. That was when she started showing me all her tricks and tips for making classic *jambalaya*, a smothering crawfish *etouffée*, or a pot of basic red beans and rice.

As I look back, I realize those lessons impacted me more than I knew. At the age of nine, I started to help put dinner on the table with my older sisters. Then before I realized it, I was cooking most meals during the week and using grandmother's family secrets—fresh garden herbs and cayenne pepper in every recipe, even dessert. Around the holidays, I learned to create her candied pecan pie with frothy egg whites and a little dash of that secret ingredient. To this day, the scents of cinnamon and cayenne are my two favorite smells, taking me back home.

I married a great guy from high school who lived right across the street from me growing up. He started riding in horse races when he was thirteen, and eventually became recognized as a Hall of Fame jockey. Kent knew what he wanted to accomplish, and nothing was going to stop him. This was a really attractive trait to me. Before marrying him, I too, was driven, putting myself through cosmetology school, while working retail, modeling, and bartending at private events. At one point, I had four jobs and was going to school full time.

We moved to California ten days after we got married and immediately wanted to start a family, yet nothing happened. For three-and-a-half years I struggled with weekly poking and prodding, medically speaking. We tried everything. I spent so many nights crying, standing on my head, taking my temperature—you name it. Nothing worked. The doctor said we had a very slim chance of getting pregnant, and that my body was not built to have a baby, so we decided to take the first steps in the adoption process. Family had always been important to me. Indeed, the thought of never having my own baby was overwhelmingly sad. As a teenager I always thought I'd grow up, get married, have kids—the traditional family arrangement.

After three years of trying to conceive, I finally let go of both the idea and the hope of having a baby. Shortly after that time, I was excited to learn from my agent in California that I had received a contract to model for *Petite Sophisticate*. Then three weeks later, surprisingly enough, I became pregnant with my first-born son after eight months of not demanding my body to do so. I was completely surprised by the news, since we were in the process of adopting a child.

When I was just eight weeks pregnant, an emergency surgery was required because I had a weak cervical wall. I was on strict bed rest for the remainder of my pregnancy; just sitting up in bed made me feel as if my baby would fall out. At thirty weeks, I decided to abandon my bed rest after hearing that my husband had been thrown from his mount during a race, and then trampled by another horse. Completely ignoring my OB/GYN's advice, my husband's business agent drove me thirty miles to the hospital in West LA where Kent had been taken.

I was wheeled up to the ICU on a gurney and positioned next to his bed. I cried. The man next to me did not resemble my twenty-two-year-old husband at all. His head had been shattered in sixteen places, and the multiple skull fractures resulted in permanent deafness in one ear. The physicians were flabbergasted that he had even survived.

I went home; five days later my water broke. This time I was taken to the hospital near our home. As a family, we looked absolutely pathetic. My husband (who had checked himself out of the West LA hospital against *his* doctor's orders) was now on a gurney next to *me*. He could barely crack open his eyes through the immense swelling in his face and head. He looked over and announced, "That cannot be my wife; that woman has four chins." It would have been nice if his comment was a result of his botched vision, but he was seeing semi-clearly. I had developed toxemia due to abrupt hypertension. Toxins were inflaming my body and had begun to attack my nervous system. I was severely swollen, in extreme pain, and in labor.

Josh was born weighing three pounds and eight ounces. All three of us were fighting for our lives. My mother stayed with me while the nurses pumped me full of magnesium, afraid that I would go into a coma. Most of my hospital stay was a blur. When I began to understand what was happening, I was terribly scared for my baby. A few days later, I was finally released, but having to leave Josh in the NICU was heart wrenching. For weeks, I returned to the hospital four times a day to breastfeed him. It was a trifecta of luck, all three of us in severe distress pulled through those difficult and painful times.

At this point in my life, when I was carrying forty-two extra pounds from the toxemia, my passion for the science of nutrients and nutrition began. It was maddening to me when I would deliberately workout six days a week, yet not see any results. Doctors prescribed medication, yet basically told me I would have to live with toxicity in my blood. They were unable or ill equipped to help me understand what was actually going on within my body.

At twenty-four, I was just beginning my life. If living through giving birth to Josh—this extraordinary gift from God—was a sign, it was saying I had to do something to get my body back and live a better, healthier life. It was up to me to learn how to heal my body from the inside out. I fought to decode and comprehend why I was in pain and feeling debilitating fatigue, as well as rampant systemic inflammation. It took time for me to figure out what to do, since the medication was not working. When I started to restore my physical structure with healthy, organic food, my life changed completely. I began detoxing my body on a whole new level and began to feel better than I had ever felt.

As far back as I could remember, my mom was always giving us weird stuff like cod liver oil if we were sick; a spoonful of cream of tartar if our stomach hurt; alum, a crystalized sulfate if we had canker sores; orange juice with lemon and whisky if we had a cold; and my least favorite, warm salt water if we had a sore throat. We thought she was just trying to torture us by giving us these terrible tasting things. Crazily enough, they always worked. These natural substances became my first experiences with holistic healing, although I didn't know it at the time.

I started cleansing my system, spending three months eating foods that would reduce my systemic inflammation. I was taking Epsom salt and baking soda baths, along with infrared saunas to increase blood circulation and rid my body of toxins. With circuit training three times a week, supplementing with daily vitamins, and engaging a different food regime, my body began to actually absorb healthy food and mineral compounds.

I gradually started to understand that nutrition is 80% of a person's health; 20% is exercise. My food consumption went from processed, canned, bagged, and boxed foods, to real one-ingredient foods that were fresh and raw: fruits, vegetables, turkey, chicken and fish. My carbs came from fruit, grains and vegetables, and I drank water, water and more water throughout the day.

Before Josh was born, my diet was horrible. My typical meal was rice with gravy, red meat, fried foods, and of course, Cajun French cuisine with lots of sauces. I never thought or realized that eating food was a way to stay healthy. If I wanted to feel healthy, I would literally go to the gym three or four days a week for a month, get to the weight I wanted, and then stop. Six months later, I would do it again!

After learning how my body worked, I became a certified aerobics instructor and personal trainer. Then I went back to school to become certified in the psychology of eating. I wanted to help others who were stuck with emotional eating. Three years later, I was so fascinated by how my body healed itself, I went back to school to study nutrition. I even competed in Miss Fitness USA in San Diego, winning third place. These were all confidence boosters for the next phase of my life.

I had always liked to work and wanted to work; however this became a huge power struggle, since my husband wanted me to be completely dependent on him. I tried explaining that this was something I needed to do for me, for my own self-worth. I sense he wanted me merely as an adornment, but that was not going to happen. I was never content to be solely the wife of a famous jockey. He was busy building *his* career, so I wanted mine, too.

Six years later, my second son, Jacob, was born without all the effort it took to become pregnant with Josh. The doctor performed an emergency caesarian this time, since my sweet boy's heart stopped while in my womb and had to be revived instantly. At birth, he was diagnosed with *hypospadias*, a congenital disorder of the urethra, and had to have eleven corrective surgeries.

I could sense there was something else wrong with my baby, but nobody believed me. I experienced verbal abuse from my husband and family when they told me, "Jacob is fine." They thought I was crazy. Finally after thirteen months of screaming loud enough for someone to hear, I proved to five ear, nose and throat specialists and two pediatricians that my child was profoundly deaf. Then it was confirmed. He had heard no sound from the time of his birth, which explains why his sense of smell was so strong, and how he could have an awareness of me when I came into his room even as a tiny infant.

Jacob was born with an extremely rare genetic disorder, Usher Syndrome, caused by a gene mutation from our chromosomes, resulting in a combination of hearing loss and gradual visual impairment. It is difficult to put into words how I felt when I found out Jacob was deaf. I definitely went through a mourning period and wanted to pull the covers over my head and not ever get out of bed. Through study, I learned there are three types of Usher Syndrome, none of which you want to hear your physician diagnose in your child. In Jacob's case, complete hearing loss, a severe balance disorder, and over time a complete loss of vision was the doctor's verdict for my precious son.

Jacob endured seventeen major surgeries in all, fourteen of them before he was five, and three more by the time he was eight. Over that span of time, I lived at the hospital with Jacob for nearly two years, as a deeper disconnect took place between my husband and me.

I didn't have a choice but to hire a nanny to care for our six-year-old son, Josh. This was very difficult for me. We had grown close as a family while living in Japan for three months while my husband rode the circuit there. It had been an incredible bonding time for the boys and me. Now to have a stranger take my oldest son to school and care for him was awful and agonizing for me. Although I was barely functioning, I did my best to have "Mom and Josh days" together. Since my oldest was such a sweet boy, he always wanted to invite Jacob to come with us on outings as well.

As a mother, it is excruciating to see your child suffering and in pain. Watching Josh cry because I had to leave yet again to take his brother to the hospital because of his seizures (that were still yet to be diagnosed) broke my heart. I was at my wit's end and at the hospital all the time.

My husband felt that all of this was taking time away from my relationship with him. I did not want to have to choose, but if he was forcing me to make a choice, it would be my sons first. I now had a special needs child that required my full attention. I tried to make us a family of four and desperately wanted the man I married to be part of my support system, but that never happened. There was never an "us."

The divorce was finalized when Jacob was nine and Josh was fifteen. My husband purposely dragged out the process as long as he could. It was really tough on the boys. He was the father of my children; we had a history together, but it was a very toxic relationship. Although it was a difficult four years of divorce proceedings, it was for the best. As a mom, my predisposition was to protect; that is what I did.

We had moved around so much with my ex-husband's job as a jockey, we went back to California on a full time basis where my boys could have some consistency with school and friends. Jacob needed stability with doctors and therapists as well, and I was able to establish a support system with a cadre of friends. Most importantly, my kids were happy.

I found out that there are two types of pain: one that hurts and one that changes you. I believe in and teach a holistic approach to health and wellness, which means that I look at how all areas of life are connected. For me healthy relationships, a fulfilling career, regular physical activity, and spiritual awareness are essential forms of nourishment. It wasn't always that way, but I had to learn the hard way. All my struggles in life have given me the impetus to go forward. I have learned to move on from what hurts my children or from what hurts me. I will never forget the lesson those years taught me.

Truly, I feel that God has given me the best gift ever—two amazing, beautiful boys. Jacob has taught me so much about life. He has never felt uncomfortable or different from anyone else. Josh is still as wonderful as he always was as an older brother.

It seems like ever since Jacob was diagnosed with Usher Syndrome at seven-and-a-half, we have been waiting for the past eleven years for "it" to happen, when Jacob would fully lose his sight. Saying we have been preparing is an understatement; I do my best daily to figure out how to give Jacob all that he possibly needs to be comfortable, happy and safe. With Jacob, I've learned it's about slowing down and letting go of all the bullshit, since that's not worth my energy. I try to enjoy the here and now.

As a mom, that means a lot of days spent leaking! I call crying "leaking," because Jacob thinks it is funny. My maternal instinct is to protect him from pain and prepare him for the unknown. I am acutely aware that Jacob gives me so much more strength than I could ever give him. He makes me laugh every day, and doesn't take life too seriously. In fact, he is constantly making fun of himself. I ask out loud all the time, "Who is the adult here?"

Josh, who continues to amaze me with his artistic ability and his many layers of inquisitiveness, drew a guardian angel knight six years ago. One year later he had a larger version of it tattooed across his upper back. On the knight's breastplate are the initials EOJ, which stand for "Eye On Jacob," the name of our non-profit foundation to support Usher Syndrome. Jacob's big brother believes he was put here on earth to take care of his little brother.

Now at the age of nineteen, Jacob will never be able to drive a car like his friends, but he wants to go to college and continue his acting career. We focus on those things together. We read and research, attend braille classes, and mostly take trips all over the world while he still has some sight, so he can have wonderful memories to keep in his thoughts before he wakes up one morning not able to see.

My hope is that I continue to instill in my two mature boys the courage to not be afraid, to get back up. I want them to try again, to love again, to live again, and to dream again.

For me, my passions continue to evolve. Holistic nutrition and healing has really changed me as a person. I am thankful for my clients; they stretch me and encourage me to learn so much more. Using food as medicine and sharing my nutritional knowledge should not be called a job—it's so much fun. But more importantly, I have accomplished my personal goals that were written in my journal years ago. I never imagined these things could happen, but they did, and for that I'm blessed.

CHAPTER TWENTY-FOUR

Joni

My courageous mother's past continues to influence my fervent interest in the empowerment of women. My vision is to amplify not only my mother's voice, but also all women's voices, both individually and collectively, helping them (and me) realize our power, understand our greatness, and model that strength for our children and grandchildren.

We all keep secrets, sometimes for good reasons, and sometimes because we are ashamed of things that happen behind closed doors. Being heard matters; it is how we turn our wounds into wisdom.

My mother has always been a giver, a pattern that most of us as women naturally adopt. Frequently, she gave at great cost to herself. For me, I want her to finally be heard here in my book, and I am proud to use her story as the final chapter.

Like so many mother/daughter relationships, ours was often fraught with misunderstanding. As a teenager, I thought she was weak, so I continually confronted her for not standing up to her second husband whom I despised. I didn't respect her choices, or support how she cowered to both his daily demands and his emotional abuse. What I viewed as a lack of self-respect agitated me tremendously. I was too emotionally immature at the time to understand the complexity of my mother's situation. I forgive her now, in hindsight.

Over the years, I began to ask intense questions of her, since I suspected buried secrets. My mother, when she was ready to face her past, provided the deep, gut-wrenching answers that I was searching for in my mid-twenties. Little did I know the silent suffering she endured as a young wife and mother. Over the years, she muddled stories from my youth to protect the image I carried of my father, who passed away from cancer when I was eleven.

As she frequently says, "No one knows what goes on inside your home until they sit at your dinner table." Our interview for this book is the first time she has fully disclosed the conflict that went on with my father over forty years ago. Throughout my life, my mother handled some of the hardest hits that life could throw at her, yet she somehow managed to spring back again and again.

The truth is that within my mother Joni, a soundless strength has always resided. In my thirties, I learned to be gentler with my judgment, recognizing she was doing what she could with what she had, and in the only way she knew how. She has always given freely of herself, without expectations, and the respect she has for others is evidenced by her desire to help them achieve their potential. Giving and accepting are my mother's trademarks of genuine caring and love.

As a mother myself, I now recognize that the job of mothering is very complex and difficult. We try to protect our family however we can, no matter what. Sometimes silence is best; other times, that same silence can be the entry into an uncommunicative prison. My mother has mentioned several times that being a mother comes with second guessing everything you're doing (or not doing), and then wondering if what you did will, in some way, scar your child for life.

I love my mother's gigantic, generous heart, along with her ability to spark up a conversation with complete strangers in a matter of minutes, a vital communication skill she has mastered over the last four decades as a hair stylist. Could this natural talent for communication have been better utilized within our family system when I was growing up? I really don't know the true answer to that question, yet perhaps most importantly, my mother is using that talent now.

Sharing our stories can always be a step toward freedom; so can making our own decisions, following our hearts, and speaking our truth. My mother taught me these realities by modeling what to do, as well as what not to do. I am full of pride and tremendously grateful as her daughter. I am also elated to be her biggest advocate, watching her rebuild not only her life, but her confidence as well.

I wasn't what you would call one of the popular girls in my high school. The "cool" status was for cheerleaders; sometimes I was jealous of not being one. But I saw myself as friendly and carefree. I could fit in with all types of people, yet never liked to draw too much attention to myself. I was a bit self-conscious and not a big drinker. You could either find me at band practice with my cornet, or in yearbook and student council meetings after school.

Tom Hogan worked at the local market, the IGA. I remember watching him bag our fruits and vegetables, being captivated by his hazel eyes. We went to the same high school, and we would flirt with each other while he loaded groceries into my mom's ivy green Ford Mustang. I started going to the baseball games to watch him play shortstop, his wavy light brown hair barely contained under his ball cap.

Tom had a big heart. Everybody loved him. He was charismatic, good looking, and the life of the party. He even drank enough Budweiser for both of us! We started going steady the fall of our junior year. I was thrilled to be going to our Spring Senior Prom together!

In the summer of 1973, the whole course of my life changed. Who knew I would unexpectedly conceive the first time I had sex, parked in the sugar beet field on a muggy summer night in Tom's two-door Plymouth. I was a wreck. Mom accompanied me to our family doctor and he confirmed my pregnancy with a urine test. The thought of telling my father scared me to death. When I finally did, he refused to talk to me for two months.

I was only seventeen. I was never taught either at home or in school about sex, let alone the need to wear protection or use contraceptives! It was a different time in the '70s. I had to learn all the "physical and emotional stuff" on my own. After the shock subsided, there was never a thought of abortion or adoption. Tom's family was Catholic and mine, Lutheran. I'm not sure if I would have considered either option even if religion was not a definitive factor. In our small town, if you got pregnant, you got married and dealt with it.

My hopes of going to college and becoming a nurse or a dental hygienist instantly came to a halt. Instead, I attended MJ Murphy Cosmetology School. The smell of perm solution fumes made me feel sick to my stomach on a daily basis; maybe it was just morning sickness. I'll never know.

We were married on December 7, 1973. To appease Tom's father and his family, the wedding was held at his Catholic Church. I wore an off-white empire waist wedding dress to hide my five-month bump, carrying an intensely fragrant stephanotis flower bouquet. Two hundred people came to the reception. I felt excited and optimistic as our real-life version of playing house together began.

Fortunately, my father's disappointment waned. He liked Tom and helped us purchase a $7,000, fully furnished, white-trimmed trailer home. We could barely afford our utility bills, but to Tom and me this prefabricated, two-bedroom structure felt like a residence for royalty! We ate boiled boloney and fried eggs for dinner on our gold butterfly Corelle dishes. From time to time, Tom would go hunting or fishing and bring back squirrel, pheasant, rabbit or blue gills for me to prepare for dinner.

My new husband was working his way up the ranks at the IGA, but he still found plenty of time for partying. At that time, it was easy for me to make the excuse that he was young, but I was, too! I found my first job at Jarvis Hair Salon in Saginaw six months later. The goal was to save up money for the arrival of our child, and we desperately needed my additional income.

Our baby girl, Shannon, arrived in April 1974.

We could have saved more money, but Tom's drinking never diminished. I had reasonable expectations of him as a father. I wanted him to stop drinking every night and stay home with his family. Then together we would navigate through the uncertainly that comes with being parents.

When he refused, my high hopes of living happily ever after with my newlywed husband and newborn child started to seem in jeopardy. Here I was, a teenager, alone, desperately trying my best to take care of the house, our finances, and a newborn without a parenting manual. Tom's routine was consistent: He would drink at the bar without stopping until he either passed out or never came home, or he would come home just *before* passing out.

Each month his behavior became more intolerable. Since I never knew where he was, it worried me sick. I spent countless hours pacing the floors in darkness with Shannon crying softly in my arms, asking myself, why am I doing this? Even as a teenage mother, I knew I had to be responsible for my actions, and I needed to be there for my daughter.

I was reluctant to accept what was happening, and was hopeful Tom would stop his childish behavior. My pride took precedence over my wisdom. My fear of failure and embarrassment petrified me. I didn't reach out to anyone since

I thought people would not believe me. I protected Tom's reputation at all costs, at my expense. I felt so alone though, never telling anyone about the situation I found myself in, stuffing my feelings deeper and deeper.

At a certain point during the first year of our marriage, Tom started to get explosive toward me when he came home drunk. My fun-loving husband turned combative the moment I asked him, "Where have you been?" I never knew what the "alcohol" was going to say or do. Sometimes I would have a mouthful of chewed-up tuna fish sandwich spit at me, or I might need to dodge a full glass of milk that would end up shattered against the kitchen wall. Retreating to my hands and knees, I would start to clean up the mess while begging him to go to bed. Yet anything I said or did aggravated his teenage angst.

Two years prior, Mom gave me one of my favorite gifts from a trip she and Dad took to Hawaii. It was a beige and white cotton caftan dress. I was wearing it one night while ironing in the living room when Tom came home in a drunken stupor and ripped it off me. I vividly remember sitting there on the navy blue tweed carpet holding my shredded dress in my hands, weeping. I continued to softly cry as I cleaned up another one of his spontaneous food-throwing fits. He finally staggered to the bedroom, where he promptly passed out.

For years, I lived in continual fear of him walking through the front door, dreading what would happen next. After so many nights of his nastiness, I decided that I would no longer wait up. My new plan was to pretend I was asleep. This idea was short-lived. My strategy failed when he pointed a shotgun to my left temple as I lay in bed one night and sternly demanded, "You always have to say something to me when I walk in the door," as he pushed the unsympathetic steel barrel against my skin.

My body trembled. My brain seized. I tried to remain calm, but his shaky right hand made me feel extremely nervous that I was going to die. I prayed to God this firearm was not loaded. My drunken, emotionless husband should not be the one to make the decision to end my life. And especially not with my little girl peacefully sleeping on her favorite Raggedy Ann and Andy doll sheets and cuddling her faded pink blankie in the next room.

I was aware of Tom's incapacity to listen when he was intoxicated, but I also knew that anything could set him off. So in that moment I asked him calmly, "Do you really want to do this? If you pull the trigger, then you have to live with that decision." He eventually put the gun down and went to bed. I ran to my little girl's room and held her as close as I could, all the while asking God, "Why me?"

What could I do now? Where could I go? Back to my parents' house? They already thought being pregnant at seventeen was an embarrassment to them. There were no services or shelters available in our small town. I could have called the police and exposed Tom's behavior, but nobody would have believed me, especially our friends and family. He never acted this crazy in front of them. Everyone liked and loved Tom Hogan.

I am not sure why I stayed after that traumatic night, but I did. I would like to confess that things settled down a bit, but as I look back, my decision was mostly fear-based. Two years after that incident, our second daughter, Shelby, was born. I did not want seven-year-old Shannon to be an only child, and it felt like it was now or never to conceive again.

Around this time, we moved out of the trailer into a house with a yard. Tom enjoyed having a garage where he kept all his "toys." Our new house was close to the IGA so he could walk to work. He seemed excited about our new place, and I loved watching him playfully interact with the girls. He was a doting dad.

Still, over time I lost whatever assertiveness and confidence I had left in me. I continued to repress my thoughts and feelings, becoming more desensitized. Tom was physically abusive to me. I didn't want to admit to anyone what was happening in my life, and, as a result, I became a victim of my own circumstances. I talked myself in circles because I was ashamed. Was I "right" to feel the way I did? Was I supposed to suffer? Everything I thought was wrong about my relationship then started to feel "right." At least I knew what it looked like; everything was familiar and predictable, which made it comfortable somehow. I thought about leaving Tom all the time, but I was trapped by my pride and fear.

I became adept at making excuses for my bumps and bruises to friends and family. I remember one particular time that tactic was a bit more difficult, though. Tom had punched me in the mouth, causing my teeth to cut through my lip.

This happened during the middle of the night, and Shannon walked in as I was hunched over a blood-filled bathtub. I told her, "Go back to bed. Mommy slipped on some ice." I lied to my friend Carleen with the same story, while we shared a green olive pizza for lunch the next day.

Tom never laid a finger on the girls, only me. He was a good dad and loved his daughters. And I know he loved me, too. But when he drank, he became a different person. Alcohol fueled an angry fire inside of him. The more he drank, the nastier he would get. Like a fire, his actions were difficult to anticipate, and when left unattended, could quickly get out of control. That scared me.

In my mind, I thought maybe it was my fault, that I was the cause of his abusive behavior. I know now that is the furthest thing from the truth, but I was young, naive and foolish. Something I regret never saying to Tom was, "You need help." His dad was also an alcoholic; like Tom, he never knew when to stop. Drinking was an accepted behavior in their family. It was also what many people did socially in our isolated community.

It may be wrong to think, but at times I wished him dead. I was angry and tired, and I just wanted Tom to stop drinking and stop hurting me. From the beginning, I was frustrated that he did not care enough to come home and be with his family. I desperately tried to remind him of his responsibilities, but that only aggravated his temper. When we exchanged vows, this was not the life I had envisioned.

There was a kind and loving side to Tom, but alcohol slithered in and stole that away. I wanted my Tom back, the one with the captivating hazel eyes who brought me home damaged cans of corn and green beans from work. Since we were always short on money, anything helped. Those little gifts meant a lot.

Shannon was nine and Shelby had turned two when Tom started having severe headaches, coupled with stiffness in his neck. The headaches were odd to me, since he never used to get them, even after his drinking binges. He visited a chiropractor and took vitamins, but the symptoms didn't get better. After developing a severe cough and seeing a physician, he was finally diagnosed with a rare form of non-Hodgkin lymphoma.

Maybe I was being young and foolish again, but I never thought about him dying, or being by myself raising two girls. I only hoped that this would be the tipping point so he would finally stop drinking.

He did.

Tom endured almost two years of both chemotherapy and radiation treatments. He was sober the whole time, due in part to the severity of his sickness. I felt like God had finally answered my prayers. This was the first time in our relationship that I saw my husband daily. I knew where he was at all times. I drove him to his chemotherapy and radiation visits. We would often stop and get Jamocha milkshakes from Arby's, which helped ease his queasiness.

Our time together began to feel like a true marriage, despite his being very ill. He would play baseball with Shelby in the backyard, and take Shannon up north to drive the quads he bought with his brother and nephew. We would go golfing together, and I would fry one of his favorite foods, either venison or fresh perch. It felt like we were renewing our relationship and starting over again. He was turning back into the Tom Hogan I fell in love with a decade earlier.

He continued to work at the grocery store when he could, and started attending a non-denominational Bible study with an old high school friend, Tony. After reading the entire Bible several times, Tom appeared calmer, kinder and more caring towards me, despite the cancerous tumor resting between his lungs on his spinal cord. This inoperable malignant growth eventually made its way into his bones, taking over his entire body.

I was sitting next to my thirty-year-old husband when he peacefully closed his eyes and passed away on August 30, 1985. A non-dramatic, eerie silence filled the room. When Tom took his final breath, part of me died with him. I was now numb and emotionally empty. We had experienced many tumultuous years of marriage. But, suddenly, my whole life felt like a bigger mess.

I had no time to feel scared or sorry for myself. I knew I had to be strong for Shannon and Shelby, now ages eleven and four. There were a multitude of bills to pay and affairs to settle. I did what I needed to do…get through each day. As long as I had my girls to raise, giving up would never be an option for me.

Thanks to my older daughter, this secret is no longer buried. I had never revisited these events until she forced me to look back and tell her about my life. It has been painful, even humiliating at times, but our conversations were therapeutic as well. Unearthing these memories allows me to finally heal that part of me. In truth, to this day I still struggle with remaining silent, not saying what I really think. I know deep in my heart this suppression is wrong, but it is a hard habit to break after a lifetime of restraint.

Now at sixty-two, I am finally taking steps toward expressing my own voice again in order to find a place of overall health and happiness. I am restoring my self-confidence, while battling type 1 diabetes. I try to visit my four grandchildren in California as much as I can, while keeping my cosmetology clients happy. My older regulars are adamant about having their hair styled on schedule—some weekly, others every six weeks.

Slowly but surely, I am finally understanding that I deserve to be happy. My daughter continues to prod, poke, and pull me to a different level of awareness. At times, I wish she would just leave me alone! Yet in reality, *her* strength has risen from *my* past weakness. That resiliency is a gift any mother would gladly suffer to give her children.

WHAT I'VE LEARNED

As a child, my paternal grandmother, Rosalie, was always reading books to me. Cuddling on the couch nestled safely under the support of her arm, I felt like she was a mother eagle protecting me in the nest. This experience of being nurtured by my grandmother—the pure anticipation of the story, the message that was encoded in the text, and the time we shared together side-by-side—left a permanent mark on my heart. We created a bond that no one could replace.

Reflecting back to those times with her, I realized they provided me with countless lessons, along with a strong foundation and belief that every story has a meaning and purpose whether it is written or spoken. Indeed, I have always felt a special closeness to all the storytellers in my life. I was forever touched by the vulnerability of the person who wanted to share a part of their life with me.

I also felt it was my duty to protect our shared experience, while absorbing the hidden lessons that could apply to my own life. It allowed me to experience a type of healing by beginning to understand that someone else had walked this path before me. This knowledge established a tangible support system for me. A personal confidant then emerged, someone who shared my same storyline, but with a different cast of characters and backdrop in their tale.

Lastly, I recognized the overarching themes that presented themselves across generational lines, and how history has a way of repeating itself. I was convinced it was my duty to learn from my foremothers' and forefathers' mistakes, not repeat them. This can only happen if the story is shared.

Consequently, as I matured and moved on into my life, I started to understand that the most important step to over-coming any self-inflicted burden was disclosure. The only way I could release myself from my emotional struggles was to allow others to witness the most complicated and hidden parts of myself. When I peeled back my layers, I noticed others were emboldened to do the same. As a result of that intimate connection, we generated a safe haven for each other through revealing an aspect of our deeper selves. This mutual openness created a "narrative medicine," something I had been searching for my whole life.

My desire to empower myself and other women was certainly rooted in watching my mother live her life from what I assumed was a position of weakness. I became passionate, sometimes overly so, about liberating her and others like her, from an habitual, imprisoned way of thinking.

Eventually, I was ready to start asking my mother tough questions. Her authentic answers brought serenity to the tired, forlorn and hurt child within me. Our time together also offered a window of freedom from a truth she had repressed for almost a lifetime.

As she slowly revealed her untold stories, I began to understand that this woman was not weak, which was how I had always perceived her, but primarily a victim of social circumstance. She constantly walked on eggshells, living in fear of saying or doing something that might trigger an aggressive response from my father. I became cognizant that she did not have the strength or courage to remove herself from the relationship. It had to be extremely difficult.

Growing up, I was aware there was tension between my mother and father. Upon hearing her life story, I learned for the first time just how intense it had been for her. She had done everything she could to conceal his alcoholic outbursts and the physical abuse that she unfairly endured over the course of their twelve-year marriage. I often still wonder if other family members saw her struggles, and why they didn't intervene or try to help. No one ever talked about the abusive man my father became when alcohol was in his veins. I have come to learn that abuse doesn't always happen overtly, and it isn't always easy to recognize. Destructive relationships can be quite covert and insidious.

Over time, and with more than a couple of therapy sessions, I realized not everyone is ready to be vulnerable at a moment's notice. I understand that more now than ever. That is one of the reasons why I wrote this book: I want to whisper quietly in your ear that you are not alone. When you are ready, you will find innumerable women to draw closer to, be in relationship with, and confide in.

I frequently asked myself how my mother could be honest without tarnishing the loving memories I had of my adored father during our conversations. I deeply respect her selflessness in keeping my remembrances pure. Yet it still pains my heart to realize she became an expert in silent suffering for the sake of other people, especially my sister and me.

I sensed that my probing gave her an opportunity to use her voice again after being silent for so long. It did. Allowing my mother to free herself, find resolution within, and step forward with a newfound strength makes me extraordinarily happy. My mother's incredible courage inspired me to want to share, heal and empower.

This book was my opportunity to do that.

What the twenty-four women featured here, as well as many others, have taught me is that we are all wounded, we all worry, and we are all weighed down by feelings of unworthiness. For me, the bedrock of love, friendship and community is vulnerability. Heartfelt exchanges can provide us with connection and consolation, since we all long to be loved, touched and heard.

Epilogue

I recognize parts of myself in each of these women, who courageously reached within themselves to overcome extraordinary obstacles. While writing this book, I've personally experienced a profound healing through telling each of their stories. Bravely, these women offer a glimpse into the rawness of their hearts so the rest of us can gain comfort and insight. My wish is that they understand how their stories have a restorative power, passing on wisdom and reassurance to everyone who reads them. We have all become experts at our own struggles, which means we all have valuable lessons to share.

I am excited knowing there are many more women who are ready to be courageous and vulnerable in conversations with me. I look forward to connecting with unimaginably brave women who are ready to expose their lives through words, if someone will listen. There was no selection bias involved in the making of this book. Every story matters, including yours!

Thank you imperfectly perfect women, near and far, for your trust in me. These narratives resonate deeply, giving us permission to liberate ourselves from suffering silently alone. Let us no longer pretend that we can do everything without help, and pretend that we have it all together. Perhaps then we can even admit that we actually do hurt. At that moment, we can decide to embrace the fact that no one has her life completely under control. We cannot choose what happens to us, but we can choose how to respond. The woman I am, and continue to become is the result of *Sharing, Healing and Empowering*.

ART GALLERY

In the process of compiling these stories, I engaged twenty-four artists to create a unique portrait that elevates each remarkable woman to a more profound level, enhancing a visual interpretation of her story. Each artist was asked to fashion a specific stylistic piece. Since several women chose not to have their actual likeness portrayed, certain facial renderings or characteristics have an abstract approach.

Every artist's representation that follows, displays a range of creative expression and experience. I continue to marvel at their surprising insights and perceptions. The artists selected and defined their personal forms of visual expression, from pen and ink, and fused glass sculpture, to traditional acrylic painting, and more.

I applaud and celebrate these altruistic artists of all ages and abilities. Without any financial compensation, each one took time out of her busy schedule to generate a rendering. I extend my deepest gratitude to all the audacious participants, since their artistry is a critical component in the overall impact of this book. Thank you one and all!

~ Shannon Hogan Cohen

ONE

KRISTEN HUBER
Dalia

"Even though I'm still in high school, when I was offered an opportunity to illustrate Dalia's story, I realized that her effort to support her daughter was nearly identical to a situation I lived through with my best friend, Olivia, one year ago. Both Olivia and Dalia's daughter, Mayra, were afflicted by non-Hodgkin's lymphoma. And each of them showed their spirit in our world after their death through a butterfly's flight. Not only was I in shock at this coincidence, it was truly a sign that my best friend was still with me. Losing someone to cancer is one of the worst pains I believe anyone can ever go through."

TWO

KENDALL GEER
Madaline

"I have a vivid memory of helping my grandma load her kiln for a firing of floral painted china one bright summer morning when I was a child. African violets lined the eastern windowsill and all was good and right in the world for me as a little girl by her side. Madaline's story deeply resonated with me and provoked those memories. Her Stanford graduation photo provided a starting point for my illustration. I was struck by the no-nonsense look in her eyes. I just knew right then, she and Grandma Winnie are kindred spirits."

THREE
BRIGITTE EDERY
Brigette

"I painted this likeness of myself right after I returned home from the hospital when the bandages came off. It was like I painted it all in one breath that day. Then I noticed after I finished it, there was an angel kissing my right eye. Do you see it?"

FOUR

PARKER LUND

Lauren

"Lauren's story was incredibly inspiring to me. Her ability to stay confident and spread positivity led me to create an image of her using pastel colors. Her calm and encouraging smile highlights how anyone can heal themselves and be strong, no matter what incredible challenges they've faced in their lifetime."

FIVE
BARBARA JEAN
Barbara Jean

"This is April, my five-year-old dark brown mare and I near a creek bed on one of the trails bordering my home in San Luis Obispo. We were both seeking a bit of security and quiet time from our daily routine. April and I always had a special trusting connection, as I was her first human friend."

SIX

JOLA

Clara

"I was particularly touched when I was asked to interpret through art, my emotional connection to Clara's story. Yet more importantly, I wanted to reiterate her message through my illustration. Thank you, Clara, for remembering and telling your life's story to us all."

SEVEN
FRANCES ELSON
Annette

"As a Holocaust survivor who came to Canada as a refugee, I have always had an affinity for people who have had similar experiences. Annette's story resonated strongly with me. She is someone who celebrates immigrants and their challenges. I see Annette as a young woman who came to a country where her spark and creativity led her to create a very successful business and a wonderful life. I feel honored to have a connection with her. I created this portrait of her using three dimensional fused glass."

EIGHT
SHARON BELKNAP
Leilah

"My illustration accompanying the heroic ongoing journey of Leilah arose from this woman's tenacity, her belief in possibility, her acute mental clarity, her physical strength, and her respect for the beautiful ongoing evolution of her soul. The colors and graphics at the base of the drawing were inspired by her culture, while the images rising up represent the organic growth of expression within the family she honors."

NINE
ACACIA ROSE PENA
Trish

"Trish's beautiful story exudes her understanding of kindness, integrity and compassion, no matter what a person does or where they come from. As a young artist, flowers symbolize growth, learning and transition for me; those are certainly a part of Trish's life as well. I drew them in her hair where I think she might put them on special occasions."

TEN

AMANDA McMAHON
Daniela

"I really felt a power and strength through Daniela's story; I knew that I had to create an expression that captured the essence of her composure and maturity. While drawing this illustration, I, too, was experiencing some rough times, so her words, *mal tiempo, buena cara,* (one must try to put on a brave face) constantly were repeated in my mind. This image with its soft expression depicts Daniela's relief, knowing that pain is only temporary."

ELEVEN
DEBBIE HUTCHISON
Julie

"Julie shared with me several photos after a race she had run, celebrating with her young daughters afterwards. This gave me the idea to illustrate her at the finish line overlooking the expansive Pacific Ocean. I wanted to show this amazing woman at the end of her race, looking back at the difficult path, celebrating that she is now a cancer survivor."

TWELVE

ANA MARIE CALANDRELLI
Suni

"My sister, Suni and I selected this portrait in pastels of her first visit from Chile to Buenos Aires, after the loss of her husband. An unforgettable healing took place for both of us when we got together at our Mom's home. We each treasure this portrait and wanted to see it printed here, so as to 'never forget how one can rise up from cinders to the light.' "

THIRTEEN
SARINA HAHN
Desiree

"I met Desiree when I was just a child. I remember actually wondering if she was human because she radiated such light and warmth. Over time, we developed our own unique relationship. The piece symbolizes how deeply Brandon still inspires his mother, and how each and every day he is with Desiree. The vision of Brandon rising up and out of the tear drops and the darkness into the light represent how, despite all the pain of what happened, Brandon and Desiree have both emerged strong and whole."

FOURTEEN
CASSIDY LEWIS
Katrina

"As a young, aspiring artist, I am completely honored to be part of the S.H.E. community and to have been asked to create an illustration, including an elephant from Thailand, for such an adventurous woman. Katrina tackled everything head on with great tenacity. It reminds me of the woman that I aspire to be."

FIFTEEN
ROSEMARY KIMBAL
Adelaide

"During our stay in Paris last autumn, my husband and I visited a David Hockney Retrospective Exhibition. When I saw Adelaide's photograph with her beloved dog, I saw an opportunity to paint her in a relaxed full smile, in a similar style to Hockney's *Woman in the Blue Skirt*. Her contented happy countenance propelled me to capture that feeling in the image in just a few strokes."

SIXTEEN

MARCEL NAGY
Linda Lee

"Linda Lee's story as a woman who has undergone a lifetime of suffering and illness, and yet forges on with her life to find love and happiness in both her relationships and her career deeply moved me. Since she worked in the Mexican tourist industry, along with having ties to Mexico, I recalled the suffering and fortitude of Frida Kahlo. Just like Frida, Linda Lee has found her own way, without complaint or apology, to embrace her life's challenges with passion and love. *Viva la Vida!*"

SEVENTEEN
DARBY HANSON
Tristen

"I chose to illustrate Tristen's story because as a holistic practitioner, I connected deeply to her transformational process. She has blossomed into a strong independent woman by following her inner knowing. I can also relate to her uncanny ability to drop the f-bomb flawlessly into any sentence. Can you find the silhouette of a woman in the tree?"

EIGHTEEN

ANITA FLAGG
Georgina

"Georgina's love of dogs speaks to my own perspective. Our pets offer us unconditional love and affection. Although we often say we are saving *them*, I really think our pets save us. *Waiting for Mom* depicts the body language of the dogs as they eagerly await Georgina's return home."

NINETEEN
SUSANNE NASON
Jessie

"Jessie's story deeply touched my heart. Her strong faith and devotion transformed her sorrows into something truly beautiful. Her sacrifices allowed her son the life she had dreamed of. I hope my watercolor illustration calls forth Jessie and Inmer's delightful relationship. May their lives continue to be filled with the beautiful blooms she labored so hard to cultivate."

TWENTY
MARIANA PEIRANO
Petra

"I usually focus on my subjects' eyes and try to capture their essence. I sensed a kindness in Petra's eyes that accompanied my brush through every stroke. I am moved and inspired by her sense of community and her passion for connections. I completely agree with her belief that food must nourish hearts and minds, as well as our bodies. I admire Petra's commitment to bring the mobile kitchens into redevelopment areas to bring life back to the streets."

TWENTY-ONE

RUTH GHIA

Ruth

"I decided to sketch myself because I still love playing around with my gadgetry after more than 60 years. I created the image on my iPad Pro using the Pen & Ink app. I also utilized the Affinity software application on my Apple computer for editing three actual photos that are part of the drawing."

TWENTY-TWO

ERICA RUSSELL

Khorshed

"I am extremely honored to be part of this project to celebrate the life of Khorshed. I am amazed at how she stood bravely against traditions that could have left her unhappy throughout her entire life for the sake of "pleasing others." Instead of being silent, Khorshed chose to break through those walls to live an abundant life of joy and freedom! I've titled this painting, *On Silence and Freedom.*"

TWENTY-THREE

LAURA RASEY MILLER
Sonia Marie

"As a mother, I was genuinely moved by Sonia Marie's story. I myself have two boys, one with disabilities. Much of my art has been inspired by my own experiences of being a mother of a child with special needs. I know that life can be challenging and ever-changing, but through it all, Sonia Marie remains an advocate and loving protector of both her children."

TWENTY-FOUR
SHELBY HOGAN KOVAC
Joni

"I hesitated when my sister, Shannon, asked me to draw our mother's image, since I was unsure of what aspect of her life to portray. The heaviness my mother has carried throughout her life is immense. The man's finger over her lips is symbolic of the past but not the present. My hope is she continues to find her voice. I am extremely delighted to be part of her journey to empowerment."

EPILOGUE
KATHY FRITZ
What I've Learned

"I stumbled upon the S.H.E. Project through a mutual friend, and immediately felt a gravitational pull to be involved with such an amazing group of strong women. We are all in this life together. To have another friend, or better yet a circle of friends to help us through both the dark and the light moments is something to be treasured."

ARTIST BIOGRAPHIES

ONE

KRISTEN HUBER
Dalia

I am now in high school, yet since I was very small, art was something that I was incredibly drawn to do—from finger painting, to arts and crafts, to doodling and sketching next to my Biology notes. Right now, I'm more than happy and very pleased where my life's path has taken me. However, last year around this time, my best friend, Olivia Malka, was diagnosed with stage 4 non-Hodgkin's lymphoma. I remember the day she called me from her hospital room at UCLA, unperturbed, and told me she had cancer. I laughed, she laughed, and we kept pretending that we were invincible. As time went on, though, everything that could've gone wrong, well, went wrong for her.

On Olivia's final day of life, her amazing mom was generous enough to let me into her hospital room. I lay close beside her, listening to see if she would say just one more thing. In the midst of all the crying, the confusion, the overwhelming atmosphere, I fell asleep to her breathing. After a time, I woke up and went home, only to find out the next day she had died fifteen minutes later. The days went on for me, then the months; the process of healing and grieving was almost unbearable. But slowly and surely, I got better. It's a blessing to keep remembering my best friend.

Instagram: @youareasaucydog

TWO
KENDALL GEER
Madaline

My grandmother, Winifred, continues to influence me both as a person and an artist. Sadly, she passed away when I was only twenty, but her flower gardens, paintings, and delicious Sunday suppers took hold of me as I've matured. Grandma's creativity and compassion enriched my elementary classroom teaching for twenty-one years. I loved inspiring my students to draw and paint, looking for ways to incorporate artistic expression into any subject matter, be it a science project presentation or rhymes to memorize state capitols. In my class, we also wrote and illustrated books, created batik designs, performed plays, and presented puppet shows.

Around my home, my flower gardens grew and expanded into a full time summer project, complete with frequent garden tours in our Colorado mountain town. During the past ten years, I've found my niche as a watercolorist. The happy surprises of water and pigment please me tremendously. I've learned it's important to pause, observe, and feel what's around us. Painting helps me do that.

THREE
BRIGITTE EDERY
Brigitte

I was born in Casablanca, Morocco and lived in Paris until the age of six. My family then moved to New York. Raised in a richly diverse multicultural environment with family roots in Algeria, Argentina, and the Berber tribe of Morocco, and strongly influenced by the French culture, I grew up speaking French, Spanish and English, traveling the world extensively. I discovered my passion for painting while attending Cornell University.

FOUR
PARKER LUND
Lauren

I am a nineteen-year-old artist attending California State University Fullerton with a goal to major in illustration, and apprentice as a character or set designer. I have been interested in art since I was very young. I take my inspiration from cartoons, anime and movies. My subject matter is usually people, and I work with traditional mediums, such as graphite and watercolor. Sometimes I will choose to draw digitally. My pieces usually consist of more muted or pastel colors. I am normally more of a masculine person in appearance and actions, but in my art I present more of my feminine side, through a round and soft feel to my style. As I continue to explore various artistic expressions, I would love to work on illustrating children's books and maybe on a television set. I aspire to bring joy to a larger audience with my art.

Instagram: @ peachi.p

Twitter: @ peachi_p

FIVE
BARBARA JEAN
Barbara Jean

Little did I know or recognize that the eons of time I spent doodling throughout my life made me feel calm and relaxed. Subconsciously, I continued this behavior when I had extra time on my hands, or when I was unable to physically get up and move about (due to my multiple injuries and recovery time) to burn off this uncomfortable feeling professionals now refer to as anxiety.

Additionally, I have always been an avid photographer, especially during the 35mm "film era." Digital photography is amazing, although it doesn't capture the beauty of movement and expression as remarkably as with a film camera. I also love to draw pictures of horses for children that need to be amused or seem sad. Horses have always been a nurturing aspect of my life.

SIX
JOLA
Clara

Born and raised in Poland, my family and I were all affected by the war even many years later. Although I never met my granddads, I had the stories and the memories. My mother was Clara's age during the war, and afterwards she made sure that we would never forget the devastation and horror. As a young child I visited Auschwitz (Oswiecim) often. It was our way of honoring those who lost their lives for our peace. WWII had no boundaries, no age limits, and no racial or religious preferences. In the end, we are all connected and affected, even more than seventy years later. Let us never forget!
Website: www.arthaute.com

SEVEN
FRANCES ELSON
Annette

Throughout my professional careers as a social worker, administrator, and interior designer I was aware of a constant pull toward my emergence as an artist at age sixty-one. I had always been fascinated by glass as a medium, and after studying several other art forms, I recognized that only glass art would provide me with the artistic challenge I needed. After a four-day beginners' workshop I closed my design business and surrendered to my passion. My work encompasses fused glass landscapes, abstracts, character portraits and mixed media pieces incorporating silkscreen, enamel and photographic images captured in glass. The emphasis is always on the brilliant colors and exciting textures that are inherent in the material itself.

My work has been featured in many group and solo shows and has been well accepted among my numerous collectors. Warm glass has given me a magic world— a world both solid and fluid, craft and art, clarity and mystery, always with an element of surprise.

Website: www.fuzionbyfrances.com

EIGHT
SHARON BELKNAP
Leilah

One of my joys in life, since my early years, has been nurturing my artistic curiosity in nature. There's plenty of opportunity for this in and around my town of Cardiff-by-the-Sea, California, and also through my travels around the world.

My love of drawing, technical ability and altruistic way of being, makes for an exciting and ever changing blend. The outcomes have been quite rewarding. One being my graphic design studio where I produce works for heart-centered organizations. Another, that I'm quite proud of, is Tidbits of Love®, an artful gift product that's fostering acts of kindness the world over. Most recently, the artwork and design of this significant and soulful book. What an honor to be a member of the S.H.E. creative team.

Website: www.sharonbelknapdesign.com
Instagram: @tidbitsoflove

NINE
ACACIA ROSE PENA
Trish

As a young artist living in Redding, California, I am particular to my artistic expression in monochromatic black and white scale. However, occasionally I do dabble in color. When I am not creating art, I work as a barista and a wedding coordinator, yet being creative and adventuring are my two favorite things to do. My friend, Cassidy, encouraged me to participate in this incredible and inspirational project and I am honored to be part of S.H.E.

Instagram: @acaciarosej

TEN
AMANDA McMAHON
Daniela

As a freelance illustrator, painter, and tattoo artist, I work under the name Amanda the Neon Savage. I am a free spirited hippie and all about being the vessel for creativity to flow through. I wish to inspire others to be creative as well. My life and art revolve around nature. Dedicating my life to my artistic craft, I am currently traveling the states with my beloved dog, Goggles.

Instagram: @theneonsavage

ELEVEN
DEBBIE HUTCHISON
Julie

I am a Southern California native, retired recently from a long career as an elementary school teacher. Besides enjoying my two young grandchildren, retirement has given me the luxury to explore my creativity through watercolor painting.

Being asked to create a piece of artwork that reflected the courageous journey that Julie has taken, at first made me feel a bit intimidated. However, after reading her story, I was not only inspired by her strength, but could relate to her experience. Like her, many years ago as a mother of two small children, I was diagnosed with cancer. I understood then how hard it is to keep a positive attitude, yet having small children helps one to not give up. I am grateful for that perspective.

TWELVE
ANA MARIA CALANDRELLI
Suni

I was born in Buenos Aires, Argentina. From a very young age, I began drawing anything that attracted my attention. I received a degree from the National Academy of Arts, *Academia Nacional de Bellas Artes*, and had as a professor, the famous painter, Ernesto de la Cárcova. After my sisters were married and began having children, my gift to the new parents was a portrait of their baby. With my older sister's nine children, and my own seven, I had plenty of opportunities to practice my art. I exhibited numerous works in Buenos Aires' art galleries, and have painted portraits of writers, spiritual leaders and world leaders. Most recently, in June 2016, I illustrated the cover of my son, Ivan Sicardi's book, *El Centinela de las Memorias.*

Email Ana Maria at Suni's address: sunipaz2013@gmail.com

THIRTEEN
SARINA HAHN
Desiree

I met Desiree when I was six years old. At the time she was dating Andrew, my dad's best friend, who had been like an uncle to me since I was born. I cherished Andrew like few others and even had a special name, "Bubba," just for him. I remember feeling somewhat suspicious when I heard he had a lady in his life, doubting that anyone could be deserving of my silly, wonderful Bubba. Yet upon meeting Desiree one sunny afternoon with Andrew, any mistrust I had harbored vanished. I grew to love the earthy smell of her curls and her goofy antics with Bubba.

I don't remember when I first heard about the death of her son, Brandon, but I do remember the shock. My respect for Desiree's strength at being so open-hearted despite what had happened was, and continues to be, enormous and profound. I look up to Desiree in many ways. Although I don't have a special nickname for her, we don't need one to know how much love exists between us. When she asked me to create a piece of art for this project, I didn't think twice. I am so honored. I am currently a student at Wesleyan University studying visual art, writing and much more.

Website: www.sarinahahn.com

FOURTEEN
CASSIDY LEWIS
Katrina

At first, creating art was a way for me to overcome anxiety, because there was something in me that needed to be expressed. Art was a place where I felt safe and understood. It was then that I realized I wanted to turn my desire to be artistic into a lifestyle.

I am a young, aspiring artist living in southern California. I have always been open to learning and designing in different art forms and mediums. I find I am constantly experimenting and playing with diverse concepts, colors and textures. In my art, I have been working toward a blend of different emotions, colors and feelings. And as an artist, I want to be someone who fearlessly confronts the objectification of women. I am currently working towards my BA degree in graphic design and business.

Website: www.cassidylewisdesign.com
Instagram @cassidylewisdesign

FIFTEEN

ROSEMARY KIMBAL

Adelaide

Contemporary Zen painting is my medium of choice. I endeavor to complete an image in the fewest strokes possible. As a proficient artist and illustrator with over forty-three years of experience, my artistic career began in 1971, when I was studying Zen and attending meditation sessions at the Tassajara Zen Mountain Center.

Using a free and spontaneous technique, my painting styles range from the traditional to the abstract. Along with illustrating ten published books, my art includes works on rice paper, canvas, fabric, scrolls, note cards, clay, ceramic tile, mosaic, film, and theatrical scenic design, and has been shown in galleries throughout the United States, Canada, and Taiwan. I live with my photographer husband, Raymond Elstad, in Cardiff-by-the-Sea, California.

Website: www.dancingbrush.com

SIXTEEN

MARCEL NAGY

Linda Lee

I received my MA in biomedical illustration and my BA in fine arts. I have worked for many years as an art teacher both in public and private schools, as well as teaching adult education classes. During my career, I have organized and executed a variety of murals, set designs and painting commissions. I currently own an aesthetic business in San Pedro, California, and I am a permanent cosmetic artist. I am also yoga teacher, certified yoga therapist, and Buteyko Breath educator.

SEVENTEEN
DARBY HANSON
Tristen

Based in Encinitas, California, I am currently an holistic practitioner. Yet drawing was my first true love—portraits in particular. I remember in grade school having to make something to sell at our bake sale, and deciding to draw pictures of people for 25 cents as my contribution. It was delightful.

Art was always my main focus in school from early on through college. I completely enjoyed creating charcoal portraits, and later acrylic abstracts. As soon as I heard about the S.H.E. Project, I knew I had to be involved. Captivated by the idea of bringing the essence of one of these incredible woman's stories to life through a portrait, I was fortunate to interpret Tristen's story.

I chose to incorporate the tree into my design, since Tristen's heart was impacted by beautiful trees throughout her travels. Now she has the intention to expand her branches to reach her highest potential and touch as many lives as possible for generations to come.

Website: ArtbyDooda.com
Facebook: Artbydooda
Instagram: @artbydooda

EIGHTEEN
ANITA FLAGG
Georgina

For years I believed (and was told) that someone could never make a living as an artist. So, I did the practical thing and studied accounting. However, after twenty-three years of working with numbers, analyzing and auditing financial transactions, creating profit and loss statements, and the like, I followed my passion and volunteered for a local animal rescue group. As the office manager there, I was able to help them with accounting, along with graphic design and photography.

Then I began taking watercolor classes, learning about technique and composition. I didn't know I could paint; I just gave it a try. Some of my favorites are landscapes of local beaches, and painting turtles and seabirds. One day, I decided to do a painting of my friend's dog as her wedding gift. People then started asking me to create portraits of their pets! I always aim to capture the animal's personality in my paintings. That's what I did for Georgina's story.

Facebook: Anita Flagg Artistry

NINETEEN

SUSANNE NASON

Jessie

I am a Canadian artist, who now creates something nearly every day of my life. Shortly before retirement, a friend of mine gave me a set of watercolor pencils. So I packed them to take with me for a winter vacation. Never in my wildest dreams could I have imagined the adventure I was about to begin, which led to an unexpected mid-life career change. The beauty of nature and the rich moments of everyday life constantly inspire me. I have illustrated several books so far, along with devoting time to lecturing and mentoring other artists.

Website: www.susannenasonillustration.com

Facebook: SusanneNasonArtist

TWENTY
MARIANA PEIRANO
Petra

My work reflects a deep concern for the human condition. Preserving the realness of emotions and expressions in the people I paint, I want to capture humanity in its true form. Born and raised in Argentina, I have spent most of my life in southern California.

My paintings and drawings are testaments to my passion for beauty in all its forms, from the sublime to the everyday. Combining my insights with modest scale, a lush yet tremulous palette, and extreme graphic sensitivity, I have recently begun to conflate the genre of portraiture (where the subject, usually a woman, is subsumed into a field of pictorial elements), along with that of traditional still life (where I situate objects at hand in delicate fields of pattern and color).

Website: www.peiranoart.com

TWENTY-ONE
RUTH GHIA
Ruth

I am a seventy-three-year-old adolescent who forgets to act her age and still likes to play with "toys." As a tomboy and the older of two girls, my mother once told me that I had only "one thing missing." I would compete with the boys in almost any sport until I turned twelve and discovered that boys didn't like to be challenged, especially by a girl their age.

Downhill skiing and designing houses have been my passion for sixty years. I built and remodeled seven houses so far, participating on most construction jobs from roofing to foundation perimeter drains and landscaping. Currently, our retirement house is on my computer CAD drawing board awaiting to be built.

I was always an artistic person, enjoying painting, sewing, knitting, pottery, stained glass, ceramic tiling and building furniture. Now I make extra time for electronic gadgets. Most of all, I love traveling and goofing off with my patient husband of almost thirty years, being with my three grown children and one granddaughter. I also enjoy having my friends and large extended family over for holidays and special events.

TWENTY-TWO
ERICA RUSSELL
Khorshed

After my college years studying art and design, I became a wife and mother of five beautiful children. Naturally, practicing my art took a back seat for two decades. In 2010 my youngest daughter, Sarah, passed away shortly after being born. Out of that tragedy God used the precious gift of creativity to bring me through a very difficult time. I began sharing my story through chalk art presentations, while also ministering to women around the USA and beyond. Currently, I enjoy teaching art to eighty students, from first grade through high school in Mansfield, Ohio.

My other passion is being involved as a Compassionate Entrepreneur with "Trades of Hope," empowering women around the world through sustainable businesses. The products are handmade by artisans who have been set free from sex trafficking and sweat shops; they now receive a fair living wage. These women are empowered to not only keep their babies out of orphanages, but also provide them with an education and a much better life filled with dignity and love.

Websites: www.RussellStudiosLLC.com
www.myTradesofHope.com/EricaRussell
Instagram: @Russell_Studios

TWENTY-THREE
LAURA RASEY MILLER
Sonia Marie

As a fine artist and illustrator, I have been painting for over thirty years. I hold a MA in painting from California State University Northridge, and a BFA in illustration from California State University Long Beach. I live with my family in Camarillo, California.

After working as an art director in the garment industry, my life completely changed with the birth of my first son, Calvin, who was diagnosed with multiple disabilities. I felt connected to Sonia Marie's story because we share that unique experience of being a mother to a child with special needs. Not only did she overcome many personal challenges, she did so while advocating for her child through helping to shape new hearing testing standards for newborns. That she was also able to pursue a career in holistic nutrition to promote healthy lifestyles is both remarkable and equally beautiful.

Website: www.studiolrm.com

TWENTY-FOUR
SHELBY HOGAN KOVAC
Joni

People tell me I am extremely enterprising, which is a trait I most likely inherited from my mother. My artistic career began when I studied Integrative Creative Arts at Western Michigan University and continues today as an Art Program Director and teacher at Holy Trinity School in San Pedro, California. For the last six years, I have coordinated an annual art show in my community, displaying hundreds of distinctive and avant-garde pieces of artwork from grades Pre-K through five that they have created throughout the school year.

Website: www.thepaintedelephant.com

Instagram: @thepaintedelephant

WHAT I HAVE LEARNED
KATHY FRITZ

I am a California-based artist whose contemplative work spans numerous mediums. I have a degree in art from Colorado State University, primarily in graphic design and photography. Discovering my passion for artistic endeavors at a young age, I was inspired by my mother who loved to draw, and by my grandmother who is an established painter. Their interest, talent and appetite for art were naturally passed on to me and a part of them exists in all that I create.

Website: www.kathyfritzphotoanddesign.weebly.com

S. H. E.

Share • Heal • Empower.™
FOUNDATION

The Share Heal Empower Foundation is dedicated
to the empowerment of women of all ages and cultures.
We will contribute our resources to promote positive change
in the lives of women through education, and
support through sponsorship.

100% of all donations received
will be invested in supporting women's
potential, power and possibilities.

You can make a contribution online through PayPal
by using the "Donate" button on the S.H.E. website:
www.ShareHealEmpower.com
or send a check to:

Share Heal Empower Foundation
1155 Camino Del Mar, Suite 116
Del Mar, California USA 92014

The S.H.E. Foundation is a 501c3 nonprofit foundation.
Thank you for your support!

ABOUT THE AUTHOR

Shannon Hogan Cohen has always had a special place in her heart for storytelling, which has provided her a safe place to listen, learn and laugh over the years. As a freelance writer, she has been published in various media outlets—from community and grassroots advocacy, to travel literature and personal narrative. Working with Hospice for ten years, serving on the Women's Legacy Fund at the Ventura Community Foundation, and starting Living Legacies Ventura County have been her most gratifying endeavors. Shannon is an advocate of women supporting women and believes stories change the world. She lives in Del Mar, California with her family.

Visit her at www.ShareHealEmpower.com

"Every woman has a story and every story has great meaning and value. By virtue of the many common threads in our stories, we realized that we are so much more alike than we are different. Kudos to Shannon Hogan Cohen for beautifully documenting the stories of twenty-four inspiring women with the intent to Share Heal and Empower. I love this book that is open, honest and real. Bravo!"

~ SHELLY EHLER
Entrepreneur/Motivational Speaker/Life Coach

"One story at a time, meet a tapestry of women imparting resiliency across ages and cultures. It will be well worth your while to set aside time to read their stories, reflect on their experiences, and imagine building a better world for future generations."

~ SILVINA RUBINSTEIN
Educator and Artist
Member of the Kauai Society of Artists

"Breaking through the silence to voice the unspeakable, these stories embody an alchemy of true listening."

~ LISA STEWART GARRISON
Social Justice Activist and Musician

"Welcome to a relevant collection of personal essays by two dozen multinational women, strong enough to be vulnerable and share their deepest struggles and triumphs. I celebrate Shannon Hogan Cohen's reminder that nobody knows what we are experiencing behind the face we share with the world. I highly recommend this book for anyone seeking inspiration and possibly, even salvation."

~ CLAIRE MARTI
Author of *Come Ride with Me Along the Big C*
and *Finding Forever In Laguna* series

Sketch Your Story

Your Story Matters

Dear Reader,

Here are a series of light-hearted prompts I used when interviewing the women. I invite you to write your own story, adding a chapter within the collected journeys of S.H.E.

Shannon ♥

- ❏ If you could choose a superpower, what would it be?

- ❏ What advice would you give your younger self?

- ❏ When has humor helped heal and empower you?

- ❏ What quality do you admire about yourself?

- ❏ Who is your Shero?

- ❏ In this moment, what are you most grateful for?

· She took a deep breath & smiled ·

_____

_____

_____

_____

_____

_____

_____

_____

_____

_____

_____

_____

_____

_____

_____

_____

_____

· She is brilliant & bold ·

Share Your Story

_____

_____

_____

_____

_____

_____

_____

_____

_____

_____

_____

_____

_____

_____

_____

_____

_____

_____

· She understands humor heals ·

S.H.E. Share Heal Empower

_____

_____

_____

_____

_____

_____

_____

_____

_____

_____

_____

_____

_____

_____

_____

· She is honest & genuine ·

Share Your Story

S.H.E. Share Heal Empower

_____

_____

_____

_____

_____

_____

_____

_____

_____

_____

_____

_____

_____

_____

_____

_____

· She is always evolving ·

Share Your Story

S.H.E. Share Heal Empower

· She is soft but strong ·

Share Your Story

S.H.E. Share Heal Empower

_____

_____

_____

_____

_____

_____

_____

_____

_____

_____

_____

_____

_____

_____

_____

_____

· She is magic in the face of adversity ·